GRIEF CHANGED MY DNA

"Daddy's Little Girl"

Sheila B. Lawson

This book is dedicated to my first love, my daddy, Eddie Bridges, AKA "Jack." I often refer to him as JB. I know that every little girl thinks that her dad is a hero. My dad was indeed a real-life hero, hands down! Both hands down! He was more than a superhero in my eyes! He was my constant, my security blanket, my advocate, my confidant, and my friend. I was blessed to have him in my life for forty years. I realize that if I had him for 400 years, I would still feel short-changed. I literally wanted him forever! I pray that I never lose sight of the memories we shared, the wisdom he spoke in his lectures, and the examples he set! Rest in Peace JB; I hope that your descendants will make you proud for generations to come. As far as what you were sent to do in the lives of your family, job well done!

To his wife, my Earth Angel, you are the definition of strength. You are the answer to so many of my prayers. Thank you for loving and caring for him in a way that only you could. You took vows for better or worse, and you endured them like a champ. Not only did you love him, but your love for us has taught me so much about the power of unconditional love. Thank you for loving me before I knew how to love myself. Thank you for being the centerpiece of this family. I could write a book about you alone! I am so grateful for you and all that you are to us. I could never repay you for something that comes so naturally to you, so that's not an impossible goal that I have set for myself. My goal is to love you for the rest of our days together and to make enough memories to last for an eternity. My prayer is that God will reward you tenfold and that his favor chases you down all the days of your life!

To my sister, we are the two luckiest girls in the world. God favored us by giving us the best father that he had in the garden to be our Dad. He is embedded into every fiber of our being, and therefore, he lives through us. There are times that I open my mouth to speak, and he shows up uninvited and his words flow out of my mouth, and I am sure you experience the same. It's a blessing to have you as a sister; you embody his demeanor. Your kindness precedes you and your generosity lingers after you leave the room. I know that this is one of the toughest battles that you have ever had to endure, and the war of grief seems to never cease, but know that I am on the battlefield beside you. May we continue to honor him, by celebrating the power of family! May the memories of him sustain you in your weakest moments and may the strength that he passed on to you empower you for the rest of your days. I love you forever.

To my kids and my nieces: my sister and I thought we were the apples of his eye, but you all came along and proved us wrong. You all were the true apples of his eye! You got by with a lot, just because he was in the room. Carry that over into your spiritual walk with God! Keep him close (in the room). Remember to share the same type of love that JB shared with your kids and with generations to come. Teach them who your grandad was and what he meant to you. For as long as we do such, he will never truly die because he will continue to live through each of us. We all have so many lessons that we learned from our "Dak-Dak," and life has a funny way of reminding all of us of the lectures that he shared. Embrace them. Recite them! Live them!

To the readers of this book, I'm certain that you have felt the heaviness of grief, and if you haven't, consider yourself amongst those who are truly fortunate. For those of you who have, know I have experienced a pain that may resonate deeply with your own. If grief ever truly diminishes, I have yet to experience it. Grief has a way of reshaping us, shaking the very foundations of our existence in ways we never anticipated. My hope is that your resilience is replenished each day through the grace of Christ. May the cherished memories of your loved ones fill the broken pieces of your heart.

Table of Contents

Chapter 1: Hey, "Boot" 1

Chapter 2: Let's Go 9

Chapter 3: You Can Let Go Now 13

Chapter 4: Dear GOD 19

Chapter 5: Don't Eat My Fries 27

Chapter 6: Be Still While It's Storming 33

Chapter 7: A Broken Heart 43

Chapter 8: It's Only a Test 53

Chapter 9: There's Nothing Left to Say 59

Chapter 10: Don't Ever Forget Me 67

Chapter 11: Broken Glass 69

Chapter 12: Small Town Girl 73

Chapter 13: Who's Report Will You Believe? 83

Chapter 14: Prepare Me 87

Chapter 15: Don't Slip Away 103

Chapter 16: What's Left to Say... Amen? 109

Part II: Life As I Have Never Known It Before 121

Chapter 17: Don't Let Me Die in This 123

Chapter 18: Grief Is too Heavy—the Aftermath 131

Chapter 19: Let's go Boot 143

Chapter 20: Don't Let Go 167

Chapter 21: Sit Down, It's Storming 173

Chapter 22: Dear GOD 177

Chapter 23: There Is Still So Much That Needs To Be Said 183

Chapter 24: Don't Ever Forget Me... 191

Chapter 25: Road to Recovery 197

About the Author.. 205

Chapter 1:

Hey, "Boot"

Grief is a monster that most of us will have to face at some point, unfortunately. We do not get to decide when or where it will punch us, and it is known to have a swing out of this world. I was forty years old when I lost the giant in my life, my dad. I never outgrew being my daddy's little girl despite my age. Even though I was forty, I somehow regressed to the five-year-old version of myself. Not only did that version of me need him, but I wanted him to hold my hand every step of the way. Pull up a chair and allow me to explain…

As a kid, my dad referred to me as "Boot." This was my nickname for way too long. Please tell me that you have been there.

At five years old, we couldn't wait to get to where we are now, but now we wish we were five years old. I was so excited when he finally dropped that nickname. I could have honestly had a funeral service to wish the name "Boot" a farewell! In one sense, I felt like the title deserved a funeral so that it could be put to rest, but also, it was warm and fuzzy and considered a term of endearment.

When I was younger, my dad didn't show a lot of emotions. I rarely recall him saying "I love you" until my teenage years. But when he called me Boot, that wrapped up all his feelings with a pretty red bow. It somehow said all the fuzzy things that he was once too stern and serious to say. As serious as he was, he felt that this little girl that he called "Boot" could do no wrong! I was spoiled to a fault. A good fault, in my opinion, but to a fault. I called my dad "Jack," his nickname, though we have no idea where it originated. His birth name was Eddie. I asked several times, but he would shrug his shoulders as if to say, "It is what it is." Which often led me to change the subject. I never called him "dad." I don't know why. I assume because I was his first child and never heard anyone else call him dad. He had a way with words, and it was never a smart idea to question him about his kids. Woe unto the person who ever asked him why I called him by his name. I have witnessed a few people make that mistake. Sarcasm was his native language, and he made sure they never asked the question again. I don't ever recall him trying to correct me in that area. He was Jack, I was Boot, and that was that! As I grew older, I would call him by his last name and, ultimately, "JB." *My* JB, to be exact.

I was born six months before JB buried his mother. I don't know if the timing of my birth strengthened our bond, being that I may have been a light for him during such a tragic time. I loved to hear him talk about the bond that he had with his mother. They were extremely close. I would like to imagine that we had a similar bond. I'm told that even during my grandmother's illness, my dad would take me over and expect her to hold me. I weighed ten lbs at birth, so I'm sure this was no easy task for her. I am delighted that we got an opportunity to meet. He would always remind me of how much I looked like her and say things like, "She knew you."

I was the youngest of my mom's four kids, and although JB wasn't their father, he adored them and he was very involved in their lives. My beautiful mom is a very strong-willed woman and the apple didn't fall too far from the tree with any of her kids. She is clothed in confidence and taught us the importance of unity. My oldest sister has always been my emotional support and my soft landing. If I'm high, she's high! If I'm in the valley, she's coming down with me. My next to oldest sister is a protector and will gladly fight a lion for those that she loves. And then there's my brother, the first person who taught me to defend myself while warding off his latest wrestling tactics. My mom and JB eventually divorced. Being that my mom had a tribe, I spent a lot of time with JB. It was just he and I until he later met his wife, my Earth Angel, and my younger sister was born.

My dad and I were like two peas in a pod, even when I was a kid. As much as I needed my dad, I can remember thinking that

I was his person and somewhat responsible for him as well. He was the strongest human I have ever known, so I'm not sure how I came up with that concept. For instance, if I felt that he would be lonely, I would cancel my playdates with my cousins to spend the day with him. This would ensure that he wasn't alone on my watch.

He was my first friend. We enjoyed each other's company. We were content, even if that meant that we were having over-boiled hot dogs for supper and sitting on the couch to watch sports, which I knew nothing about. He would kick back and yell curse words at the players as if they could hear him. I would over-indulge in all my favorite snacks that were lined up on the couch. He had a sweet tooth, just like me, and knew how to keep me quiet. Every so often, he would look over at me after yelling his choice words at the players and say, "You ok, Boot?" I would nod and continue stuffing my face until I went off to sleep. He would pick me up, tuck me into bed, and quickly (I stress quickly) give me a goodnight kiss on the jaw. Remember, he wasn't a man that showed a lot of emotion. His actions spoke for him. All was well in my world at that very moment. There was no safer place that I could think of.

One of my earliest childhood memories is of me memorizing his work telephone number. I called him for *everything*. Lord knows, I must have called that man's job at least five times a day. The receptionist would answer the phone and simply yell down the hall, "Jack, it's Sheila." That's me, I'm Sheila. No my name is not Boot, but as much as I wanted to drop that name, I was kind of offended that she called me by my birth name. Who gave her permission to call me by a strange name when speaking to my dad? I wanted him to check her and tell her my name was Boot! I know that's weird, right? It was the name I didn't want but expected. Or maybe I even needed it in a sense. She wasn't worried about what my name was. I'm sure she was thinking, "Jack, would you please tell this child to stop calling here?"

Instead, he pretended to be just as excited as I was. He would come to the phone and simply say, "Hey, Boot," as if I hadn't called just an hour earlier. I was calling to check in and make sure that he was ok, so I would think of any stupid excuse to call.

I would say something like, "Can you stop and get me some chips on the way home?" He did that every single night, so I'm sure a reminder wasn't necessary. He would stop nightly to get me a bag of barbecue chips and a lollipop for snack the following day. But instead of saying, "Now you know I'm going to stop and get the chips, why are you calling?" he would simply reassure me that he would not forget. If cell phones had been invented back when I was calling his job, he wouldn't have stood a chance. But he had a way of ensuring that I never felt like a burden. He answered every single call for as long as he lived.

My dad would not say goodbye when the phone calls were over. He would simply hang up the phone when he assumed we were done speaking. He would literally just hang up the phone. Don't worry. If I had more to say, I would call back. I still remember the first time I tried that. My dad never said no to anything; if the answer was no, he would give alternatives. There was one time I called his job, and he said no, and I was crushed. My heart was broken. I drew a blank and did what he had done a million times when the conversation was finished: I disconnected the call. If he were here, he would say that I hung up on him, but I don't believe that was the case. I never received a whooping, but my dad drove all the way home from work that day. It was not common at all back then to go home on a lunch break. He worked the second shift, and I was usually in bed before he got home at eleven p.m. I heard his car pull up shortly after the phone disconnected, and I just knew that would be the day that I would get my first whooping. Instead, he gave me what felt like an eight-hour lecture. I mean, you really would have thought that I killed somebody.

When he arrived, I was sitting at the bar overlooking our kitchen. This was one of my favorite spots because I loved to spin on the barstools, and the rotary phone hung on the wall next to me so that I could continuously call his job. I hung my head and pretended to be engrossed in homework when he sat in the seat next to me. He cornered my stool so I could no longer spin and leaned in to ensure that I was at eye level. He looked me right into my big ole eyes and went into a lecture that seemed to last a lifetime. Surely his lunch break was over, I thought. That receptionist had to be looking for him at work! He would usually melt over my tears, and of course, they did begin to fall as he continuously recited how that better not happen again. Each teardrop that rolled down my face seemed to be huge. He softly caught each of them before they reached the edge of my chin, but it didn't stop him from talking. He made sure that we were on the same page.

I learned to say goodbye, even if he didn't. It taught me that the final goodbye was important to him. It was something that he needed to hear. I never made that mistake again.

The very next day, I resumed calling his job as scheduled. Besides, he always made sure we were good after a lecture. If I couldn't think of a reason to call, I would just tell him that one of my older siblings had done something to me—when they had not. That was his pet peeve and I learned early on that this was an easy way to get him to come to my rescue. I confessed this tactic well before he died, and we would laugh about it. My siblings, who were aware of the tactic the entire time, can all laugh about it today as well. He would say, "I don't put my hands on her, and no one else will either." I can still hear him yelling at them to keep their hands to themselves, then turning to me to say, "Come on, Boot, let's go!" I thought to myself, mission accomplished. Those were the days! He has rescued me for as far back as I can remember. I would give anything to hear those words today, "Come on, Boot, let's go!"

Chapter 2

Let's Go

Besides spending an evening watching my dad yell at the TV screen, it was not unusual for him and I to hang out doing absolutely nothing. I was born in a small town called Milledgeville, Georgia, during an era in which people took joy rides just for fun. The town was so small that there weren't many places to ride. Needless to say, that gas had to have been much cheaper back then. My dad owned a 1977 XR7 Cougar. Now, his family had a special place in his heart, but I am not sure that we could compete with that car. He loved that car. I kid you not, my dad washed his car every other day, if not every day. It had a silver custom paint job with glistening sparkles and boy did he make sure they glistened. Red was my dad's favorite color. The cougar had a beautiful red cloth top. He took so much pride in that car; not only did he ensure that he shined it up frequently, but he also ensured that people would hear the car coming well before they saw it. He also had an undeniable love for music, old school music from the sixties and seventies, to be exact. He would blast the music as loud as it could possibly go. I would look forward to a ride with him once he finished washing his car. We would circle the same blocks repeatedly. We would hit all the major spots that his friends hung out at, but never for long. My dad never stayed anywhere long. Thankfully, when introducing me to his friends, he introduced me as Sheila and not Boot. But most of them would call me "Lil Jack." All his friends knew me, but each time we saw them he would do a formal introduction. We were typically only there long enough for them to admire his car before we would ride off into the sunset. Now that I think about it, gas must have been dirt cheap. There were a lot of joy rides in our past time.

Playing cards was one of his hobbies and he took the game very seriously. Card games were on set days, which were the 1st and the 15th of the month. Typically, I didn't attend those unless it was at his cousin s house. He did more yelling during those card games than he did while watching sports. In between games, he would peek in on me and ask, "Are you ok Boot? You haven't eaten all of your snacks, have you," before quickly returning to the game. I never stayed up long enough to recall us going home. The card games lasted well into the night. My feet never hit the ground when we left. I would wake up the next day neatly tucked in bed. I wonder if he turned the music down for the ride home.

My dad wasn't a flashy guy, well, maybe he was on the first Sunday of the month. That was the Sunday that he would typically attend church, with his tailored suits, socks that were so stylish that they were sure to catch your eye, and finally, a flashy watch from his collection. He would make sure that you could see his watch. He would check his timepiece even if time wasn't important. If you made mention of his watch, he would smile from ear to ear. He had such a beautiful smile, but because he was a man of very few words, many did not realize it. At first glance, you probably would have thought that he was mean. He also dressed up daily for work. He worked at a psych facility as a health service technician, so I'm not so sure why he dressed as if he was the CEO of the organization. He would put enough starch in his clothes for them to stand up by themselves before he stepped foot into them. So, besides work and church, he was pretty lowkey. But he ensured the car was always flashy. He would refuse to drive down dirt roads. If the road was not paved, you could rest assured that we were walking, no matter how far it was! He would pick me up and carry me like I was only five pounds, and I was double that weight at birth. He would park the cougar wherever the pavement ended, and you would walk the rest of the way. He would always park far away from civilization, as I would call it, so no one would park beside him. We were always in the very last parking space. Did I mention that he loved that car? Ok, I think you get the picture.

My dad's presence was always my safe place, so despite how loud he blasted the music, I was usually asleep two to three minutes into the car ride. Looking back, I sometimes wonder if he took those rides to put me to sleep. Nevertheless, I would wake up to him tossing me over his shoulders like a ten-pound bag of cornmeal. He desperately tried not to wake me. This went on for at least ten years and I wasn't a small kid. Our rides usually included a stop by the local grocery store for a case (never just one) of creamsicles. This lets you know that I wasn't a small kid. I could never stop at just one, and being the spoiled brat that I was, JB allowed me to continuously eat them. That was my JB, and he didn't believe in half doing anything. He surely had a "go big or go home" mentality. If I asked for a lollipop, he would buy me three. He was a provider for sure. He enjoyed making others smile, especially his kids.

I can still smell those days of my childhood! It smells like peace. I do realize that peace is not a smell, but it describes the smell perfectly. It smells like the sun in its brightest hour. It also smells like Armor All on the leather seats of that Cougar. It smells like my dad's cologne mixed in with sweat after he finished washing the car. It smells like creamsicles. It smells like a safe place that I can only revisit in my mind, sort of like my favorite hiding spot. It smells like the nickname "Boot" that I would take back in a heartbeat. The only way that I can describe it is that it smells like peace.

Chapter 3:

You Can Let Go Now

One of my fondest memories of my childhood was of my dad teaching me to ride my bike. Learning to ride that bike was a major move for me. I was never allowed to step foot into the street before that moment. To say that I was excited is an understatement! JB had begun hyping me up on the ride home by telling me that he had a huge surprise for me. This was new and unusual. He wasn't good at keeping secrets. I would typically know exactly what I was getting for my birthday or at Christmas. He would allow me to pick out the gifts to ensure that I had what I wanted. Our town was so small that we did a lot of our Christmas shopping at an auto parts store that had a selection of toys in the back. Looking back, he must have had some form of credit with this store, and I took full advantage of it. The workers knew him by name, and they obviously knew that I was a brat. After greeting my dad, they would quickly point me in the direction of the latest and greatest toy selection that they had. I was always like a kid in a candy store whenever we visited. I don't recall many surprises from my dad, but this day was different. He simply said, "I have something for you when we get home." My mind immediately began to wonder. I was certain that it would be a new box of creamsicles. To my surprise, it was the most beautiful bike I'd ever seen. I didn't pick it out, so that meant a lot for me to think that it was beautiful. I was somewhat picky even as a kid which was why JB let me select my own gifts. But he did a good job. It was three times my size but was pretty with all of the bells and whistles attached. Remember, he believed that bigger was better. He never bought things to fit my current size. His thoughts were that I could grow into it. But oddly enough, he bought me a bicycle every single year until I was in the eight grade. So, I didn't really have an opportunity to grow into the "big bike" before I had an even bigger one. I remember thinking to myself- that he thinks too much of me if he thinks that I can ride this big ole bike.

My dad had a way with lectures that I didn't learn to appreciate until later in life. These lectures lasted for weeks, months and sometimes years. While teaching me to ride a bike, it was no different. If I didn't do things the way that he explained it to me, you can bet your bottom dollar that we were going to have a very long conversation about it. A *very* long conversation. By the time it was said and done, I could recite the lecture word for word. The lectures were never a one-and-done. And I do mean never! My dad did not believe in spankings, so I guess the lectures were his alternative. My cousins thought that I had it made because I didn't get spankings. I thought that they had it made because once they got a spanking, the ordeal was over, and there was no need to talk about it anymore. That wasn't the case for me.

Early in life, I learned to tune them out (or so I thought) because again, he would revisit the same instructions. I was a "know-it-all" even as a kid (I forgot to mention that part earlier). I was not wiser than my JB by any means. He knew those seeds of his lectures were not falling on deaf ears, no matter how hard I tried to tune them out. Maybe there was a method to the madness of repeating them after all.

JB and I made our way to the street with the shiny new bike. Just as with anything else that was new, he began to recite the instructions of what I had to do once I was on this "big girl bike." He stressed how confident he was that I could do it. He also elaborated on the fact that I myself had to believe that I could do it. Meanwhile, I was busy trying to convince myself, "I got this." He was in full lecture mode, but the whole time, I was talking to myself in my head saying things like, "Just try not to kill yourself, Sheila!" "You can do this Sheila." My thoughts were, if he expects me to ride this big bike in the road, then surely it's time to call me Sheila. Needless to say, we had two full-blown conversations going that were very different. So, as per usual, we did a few trial runs as my JB would walk alongside me, holding onto the big girl bike still reciting what I needed to do in order to ride it all by myself. I was content with the idea of him holding on to the seat forever while I pedaled! That idea surely made perfect sense to me since I could barely reach the pedals.

Then he said, "Boot, you gotta learn to ride without me holding on," and the world paused. Who did this guy think I was? Why would I ever need to ride without him holding on? He continued talking, but by now the voices in my head were much louder. His conversation was interrupting the conversation that I was having with myself, and I was getting all confused. He was trying to get me to brace myself for the road ahead. And I was just trying to survive the moment. I knew that I was safe in that moment simply because he was holding on. I knew that if he were within reach, he would catch me before I could fall.

I can still remember the day that he finally let go! I was doing it. I was pedaling my little heart out. I was balancing! I was doing great up until the point that I noticed that his voice had become distant. I turned completely around to see him standing in the middle of the road with the biggest smile on his face screaming, "You're doing it, Boot!" Immediately I crashed! I mean I crashed full force! If there was such a thing as an epic failure, this was it. The tires continued to spin, although I wasn't pedaling, and it felt like my pride was somehow caught in the cycle. I promise that if I could have fought that bike, I would have. Suddenly, my shiny new toy had become my enemy. I lay on the pavement in fetal position crying a river as JB did a short sprint to rescue me. If only he were closer, I never would have fallen, I thought.

He scooped me up from the ground as only he could. As he pulled me in his arms, he said, "It's alright Boot; you're ok," while drying my tears. He hated to see me cry. Once the tears stopped flowing, he immediately went into lecture mode. "Boot, I have to eventually let go of the bike; you're a big girl now," he said. I wasn't sure who told him that, but we were not on the same page. I had somehow missed the memo! In that moment, I was okay with being "Boot" for a little bit longer if that meant avoiding that bike! Did I tell you that his lectures lasted for weeks, months, and sometimes years? Well, this time was no different. He talked about how I had to focus on what I was doing and ride from the time we woke up in the morning until the time that we "hit the hay sack" at night, as he would say. In other words, until we retired to bed. Before long, we were back on the pavement practicing again. Somehow, the idea that the road was a dangerous place seemed more realistic to me. At this point, I would have been ok with practicing in the grass. "Nie, you can't turn around and look at me. Focus on what you are doing; just keep pedaling," he recited over and over again! I was as nervous as I could be! I didn't want to let him down. But I didn't want to hit that pavement again either. One day, out of nowhere, I screamed, "You can let go now, Jack!" I don't even know where it came from. It was like an out-of-body experience. Who was this kid? Who gave her permission to say that? What changed and when? This was a new form of bravery that I hadn't known previously. I opened my mouth and somehow those words came up from my belly. Although he told me not to look back, I did it anyway. He was a few feet behind me. It was at that time I realized that he had already let go!

Who gave him permission to do that, I thought. He knew that the timing was right. He knew I was ready! I only had a split second to think before I had to refocus. It only took me one fall to realize that the pavement did not play fair. Immediately, somehow, my personal conversations with myself ceased. His lectures had somehow overpowered them, and now I was reciting his instructions to myself. Just keep pedaling, Sheila, and focus on what you are doing! Look at me reciting the lecture that I once tried to ignore.

There was no turning back after that. It was a daily routine to ride that bike down what seemed to be the longest road ever. He would stand at one end of the road while I would race as fast as I could up and down the road. I would often look back to make sure he was still there watching with the same prideful smile. I recently visited that old road and its funny how different it looks as an adult. It literally looks as if I could jump from one end of the road to the next now. How could that be? I was once pedaling my heart out trying to survive and make it from one stop sign to another as a kid. Before I learned to balance the bike, this road seemed as long as the Nile River. Surely, the road shrunk over time. Or could it be that I simply viewed it as a giant? A giant that I defeated simply by saying, "You can let go now."

Chapter 4:

Dear GOD

Just as my dad took pride in detailing his car, he also took pride in maintaining his mother's grave. He would routinely pluck the surrounding weeds and keep it swept and freshly painted. Our joy rides in the cougar often lead us to her gravesite. I have no recollection of my grandmother; remember, I was only six months old when she died. However, I enjoyed sitting at his feet and listening to stories of when he was a kid. He had three sisters. He was the only son that his mother had. He spoke very highly of his mom, and you could tell that he loved her dearly. You could also tell that the pain of grief still ran deep within him when he spoke of her. As a child, dead people were my biggest fear in the entire *world*! But I knew my dad needed me, or so I thought, so, I would put on my big girl pants whenever we went to the graveyard. I knew that I was safe next to my giant. Besides, I wasn't taking any chances of being left behind anytime he would crank that Cougar up, no matter the destination.

It was always scorching hot when we went to the cemetery. My grandmother was buried in the country. Imagine that "the country" within an already small county town.

I was one of the biggest sleepyheads in the world as a kid. I napped so much that one of my aunts called me Rip Van Winkle (The short story by Washington Irving about the guy who slept for twenty). So, needless to say, I would be asleep by the time we reached the gravesite. But as soon as the car music stopped blaring, I would jump up to check on JB. I was so scared of that graveyard. Despite my fears, I would jump out of the car just to stand in his shadow. Maybe I was too afraid to stay in the car alone. But either way, whatever we had to face, we would face it together.

After completing his duties, we would climb back in the Cougar that smelled of Armor All. He would blast the music before we even left the church grounds. The music was loud enough to wake the dead for sure. I would stretch out on the seat with my head resting right at the base of where he was sitting and stare into the bright sunlight until I quickly drifted off to sleep. His choice of music wasn't my favorite; I guess I was too young to understand it at the time.

I spent a lot of time with my aunts, my dad's sisters. One of my aunts kept me in church and taught me to pray at an early age. So, I have talked to God for as long as I can remember. I would always pray for my dad. The trips to the graveyard showed me that my dad had to live without someone that he loved dearly. I immediately became consumed with the idea of having to live without him someday. I was trying to understand why people who once walked the face of the earth were now covered by a cement slab. My dad would randomly say things like, "When I die, I want to be buried here next to my mom." That was a topic that I didn't want to entertain.

I thought to myself, "Sir when you go, I m going with you!" So, I resorted to what I knew and that was to tell God what I wanted in prayer. I began telling God that I did not want to live without JB. Don't get me wrong, I have never been suicidal; besides, I was only five years old or so. But living without my dad seemed merely impossible to fathom. Not only did I tell him what I wanted, but I also told him how he could do it, just in case he needed help from a kid who thought she knew it all. My prayers went something like this, "Dear God, if you ever decide to take my daddy; please take me with him. You can take us in a car wreck while taking one of our rides; I just don't want to live without him!" I know you are probably thinking, sounds scary, right? But I have always served a wiser God! My dad would have sho'nuff been upset if he had known that I was praying against that Cougar! That would have led to a lecture for sure! Thankfully me and my dad were never in a car wreck together, but he did crash his precious Cougar one time. As a matter of fact, he crashed it a couple of times. And guess what? He went and brought an *exact* duplicate. He even repeated the same paint job. He changed absolutely nothing. I forgot to mention that the car had small script on the side that read "Eddie s Love" embedded in the paint. I told you that this car was the prize, so how dare I speak any harm over that car in my prayers!

I know adults often say that kids don't worry, but I disagree. I worried about my dad. I worried that he would be buried next to his mom someday, and I would be left here alone. I worried that maybe he would be lonely if I was away. I worried if he got home too late. I just always worried! It was just me and my dad for what seemed like an eternity. I can still remember when he introduced me to his "friend at the time" (his eventual wife). He referred to everybody as a friend. You could be dating someone for five years, and he would ask about "your friend." He never addressed anyone as a boyfriend/girlfriend. If it wasn't a husband/wife, it was just a friend in his eyes. So, he introduced her to me as his friend, but I knew better even at my young age. I thought that she was the most gorgeous woman ever. Her hair stretched down her back; it wasn't coarse like mine. As we would say in the African American community, she was high yellow! Her eyes appeared to be a different shade of greenish/gray every time I saw her! She was very softspoken. She didn't have any kids. As soon as she left, he asked me what I thought. I shrugged my shoulders. Besides, why did it matter if she was just a friend? The only thing I can remember thinking was if she thought she was going to steal my JB, she had another thing coming! I am sure that they both could tell that I was super clingy anytime that she came around. Don't judge me; remember, I was just a child. Even as a child, it took time for people to grow on me. Not much has changed in that area; this is still the case today. God blessed her with an extra dose of patience. He didn't give me and JB much of it at all. If he did, we must have forgotten where we placed it. She lived in a neighboring town called Sparta, Georgia, and as a child that seemed so far away. The trips to her house would take just as long as the trips to the graveyard, if not longer. But my trips with JB were never about the destination; they were all about our journey.

My dad worked the evening shift and would get off at eleven p.m. each night. He had one day off during the week and was off every other weekend. I probably knew his schedule better than he did. I was a very scared kid. The weird thing is, I was afraid of the supernatural; I wasn't afraid of humans. I would imagine things like someone coming out of the graveyard that we visited to snatch me up in the night. He didn't like it if I was still awake when he got home. Most nights, I would just spend the night at my aunt's if he had to work. She had kids my age and they were my very first best friends. They also did a pretty good job protecting me from the graveyard bandits that lived in my head. My three aunts were all neighbors. My dad and I lived with one of his sisters and the other two lived across the street. We spent a lot of time at each other's homes because those were basically the only places that we were allowed to go as kids. Even if I spent the night across the street, I still would have to check in on my dad, or at least that s what I told myself. I destroyed every pair of window blinds my aunt purchased. She was the rich auntie with a long-paved driveway. This is important to share because although we lived across the street from her, our driveway wasn't paved. JB wasn't parking his cougar in a driveway that wasn't paved under any circumstances. He made his very own parking lot at the end of her driveway, and he would walk across the street to go home. My cousins and I were supposed to be in bed by nine o clock, but as much as I loved to sleep, I couldn't rest until I knew that JB had parked that Cougar outside. I would develop a peek hole in her blinds to see if he made it home.

On some nights, as my cousins and I prepared for bed, I would notice that my dad wasn't home by 11:20! Each night, he would stop by the convenience store near his job to get me a snack for the next day. I would give him twenty-thirty minutes of leeway to get home before the worrying would kick in. I had the trip mapped out. If he was not home by 11:30, I just knew that he had slid to Sparta to see his pretty "friend" as he would say. Or maybe, just maybe, the wreck that I had planned out for God had somehow happened without me. The only exceptions were the 1st and the 15th of the month because those were the nights that he attended his card games. Any other night, I would call his job to verify. Luckily, a new secretary would answer after the shift had changed. Thank goodness, she wasn't aware that I had likely called all day. She would politely let me know night after night that he had already left.

My favorite cousin would struggle to stay up with me while we patiently waited. We would pretend to be sleeping so that no one caught on to our shenanigans. It wasn't long before her "pretending" was followed by snoring and I would have to nudge her to wake her up. Besides, I wouldn't be able to fight off the bandits alone. She would see the worry in my eyes and desperately wanted to go to sleep, so she would ask, "Do you want to pray again"? We had already done our traditional "Now I lay me down to sleep" prayer prior to climbing in bed. We would take turns peeking out the window while destroying the blinds. She was tired of me jumping up to look out that window, but she knew me well enough to know that I wasn't going to sleep before he arrived. On our knees we would go, reciting the words, "Dear God."

Before long, I would hear his music ringing in my ears, well before I saw the headlights of the Cougar turn into the driveway. I would exhale a deep sigh of relief. I would do my final peek being careful that he didn't notice me. He would get out of his car with the brown paper bag of snacks. The snack was always the same, a bag of chips and a lollipop. He would circle the car. I m not sure if he was admiring it or if he was checking to make sure that no one had damaged it on the way home. But he did this nightly. Once the cougar passed his inspection, I would watch him cross the road to go home. Only then was I able to hit the hay sack for the night. I would whisper, "Dear God, thanks for listening!"

Chapter 5:

Don't Eat My Fries

If I was lucky, my dad and I would stop for hamburgers after taking one of our rides around town. He didn't like to eat at my favorite burger joints. Or at least that is what he would say. Most of the time, we would grab me a kid's meal to take home so that he could catch some form of sports on television. As for him, on most nights he was just fine with boiling himself a hotdog before the sports game started. But on this particular day, he decided that we would dine inside and it wasn't even my birthday. My dad was not big on crowds or interacting with strangers, so dinner at home was a good fit for him. I was excited to dine inside but worried at the same time. This time, the worry was different; I was worried because my dad didn't order food for himself. The idea of two people dining inside with only one meal did not add up for me. What was he going to eat, I wondered. I feared that I knew what would happen—he would eat some of my fries! He asked me to pick out a seat for us. So, I found the perfect seat. I was a know-it-all, and strangely enough, he encouraged it.

For instance, he would feed into the idea that no one could have selected the seats the way that I did. And I believed him. He made me feel like the queen of England or at least the smartest kid in the world. Back then, the kids' meals were still in the neat little boxes. Those were the good ole days. I had to be around eight years old. And yes, I was still eating a kids' meal! I would unravel the prize included in the meal before eating the food. I can still see him holding my right hand as clear as day now (I'm left-handed), so the left hand was busy. For the life of me, I do not recall the conversation. This does not surprise me since I had mastered tuning out the lectures. I wasn't in trouble, so I didn't understand what there was to discuss. I do remember him asking "Is the food good, Boot?" He always asked that though! I was more focused on his free right hand, constantly grabbing a few of my fries at a time. He didn't like the burgers, but he obviously liked the fries. He asked me how I would feel about having another sister (I already had two older sisters by my mom). But honestly, that's all I remember! I don't even remember my response. What I wanted to say was *can you stop eating my fries*? That's all I wanted to talk about. If my dad were here today, he would say that he told me on that day that I had a younger sister. I cannot confirm or deny it because I was focused on the fries. My dad was known to be very detailed in his lectures, but I think this lecture was a one-liner. This wasn't a lecture by far; it was a one-and-done. To my surprise, I met my baby sister shortly thereafter. Remember I told you how pretty my Earth Angel was, well, my sister was just as pretty. She was the fattest baby that I had ever seen in my life, and she was now the apple of his eye as well. You would think that I would have been jealous after being the only child for so long. But honestly, I don't recall feeling jealous at all. I think that I probably got that out of my system while adjusting to Earth Angel. And besides, I think both JB and Earth Angel over-compensated to ensure that I felt included and that both my sister and I knew just how much we were loved.

Time seemed to speed up around that time, or maybe my memory just became clearer as I aged. But I can still remember us house hunting and ultimately moving into our first home for the four of us! In the new family home, I had my own big girl room. We didn't live far from my cousins, but they were no longer across the street. So, I couldn't run over and convince them to let me sleep in the middle if the fear of the midnight bandits arose in me! That fear arose much more frequently than I care to admit. My baby sister was fearless however! She had her own space that she was so proud of, even after dark! She was a lot braver than me. I loved the thought of having my room during the daytime, but I was highly convinced that something supernatural was coming to get me after sunset. I don't know if it was a tactic for my dad to scoop me up just as he did when I hit that pavement while learning to ride my bike or not. My dad was a superhero; he did just that anytime that I was scared. Until this day, I am not sure of what I was so fearful of, but whatever it was, it had me in a chokehold. This fear was not as evident when I was with my older siblings or with my cousins because there was always someone there to protect me. Of course, it was never evident when JB was in the room. Having him close by always made me feel safe and diminished any possible fears.

I often wonder why no one addressed the elephant in the room and asked me what in the world I was so scared of. It wasn't a secret. Everyone was aware of it. I m not sure that I would have been able to explain it either way. And JB probably would have shot the conversation down with his sarcasm. He was very protective. I do recall him saying that I got it from my momma. But she wasn't as scared as me, and in JB s eyes, it had to be somebody s fault, so I guess she caught the blame. If I had a sleepless night, I would call my dad in the middle of the night and he would come and get me, whether I was in the next room, across the road, or across town.

I honestly don't know how Earth Angel tolerated my unintentional shenanigans. Anytime that I got ready to spend the night somewhere (which only consisted of two places), JB would sit me down for a lecture to see if I was sure that I wanted to stay overnight because he *was not* coming out in the middle of the night to get me if I was scared. This had happened more times than I could count. I would simply nod like a big girl to let him know that I was positive. I would gather my things and head out with every intention to survive the night. But he knew that he was coming if I called, and I knew it too. Somehow, I would wake up during the middle of the night, and although I was surrounded by people, I was still scared. This rarely happened at my one auntie's house. We were usually exhausted by the time we went to bed. But if I happened to wake up, my favorite cousin would eventually wake up with me and we would make our way to the kitchen for snacks until we crashed again.

On those occasions that the mission failed, I didn't hesitate to make that call in the middle of the night. He would pick up the phone without the traditional "hello," he would simply say "Here I come, Boot." My dad did a lot of walking, most of it for exercise. For some reason, he would choose to walk to get me in the middle of the night. We now lived about a mile away from our family. Either he didn't realize how scared I was or he didn't want to wake the Cougar, but in my mind, it took him too long to get there. If only he had driven, he would have gotten there much quicker. It didn't take a know-it-all kid to figure that out. He wouldn't say a word when he arrived; besides it was too late at night for lectures. It was pitch black outside. I couldn't even see my hand in front of me if I tried. Despite the darkness, I was no longer scared because my daddy had arrived. He would say, "Come on, Boot," as he scooped me up onto his back. I was fast asleep within minutes of starting the journey home.

My dad lectured me about a lot of things, but we never discussed my fear. He never voiced that he expected me to be brave or strong in that area. He never mentioned it. Contrary to when I learned to ride the bike, he didn't encourage me to be a big girl in this area. He knew that I would call on him, and we both knew that he would rescue me.

Chapter 6:

Be Still While It's Storming

As previously mentioned, I spent a lot of time in church growing up. The name of our church was Oak Grove Baptist #1. The number one in the title was important. I thought that this meant that I had the best church in the world. At that time it was a very small sanctuary. We later built a larger sanctuary next door. But I have a lot of sweet memories in the old sanctuary. My cousins and I would sit along the back row of the church when we were not in the choir section behind the pulpit. The children's choir sang on the second and fourth

Sundays. On the alternate Sunday, we would race to get our seats in the congregation. The benches and the floors were made of wood. This was exciting because we sang those hymns as if we had experienced life. We would stomp our feet on those wooden floors and hit on the benches while we sang along. This was music enough to our ears, despite how we may have sounded. My auntie sat up front on the second row or so, but all she had to do was tilt her head in our direction if we were getting out of hand and we knew to straighten up and fly right! She had four kids of her own, and I was like the fifth, as I tagged along as often as possible.

I have never been able to sing; none of us could really. But I have always loved singing. We enjoyed singing in the choir. When we finally got our choir robes, we took our singing to another level in our minds. We would rush home to practice after learning a new song. At home, we would pretend that we were the lead singers using anything as a microphone.

I remember when my favorite cousin and I led our first solo! I guess the choir director could tell that we did everything together. The two of us were always getting into devilment together, so we figured that we might as well stand side by side and do something for the Lord together! The fact that we would do it together gave me strength. The song was pretty simple and we were expected to only sing a few lines. Our lead lines explained to the Lord that we needed him. We practiced that song coming and going for months. Someone was finally taking a chance on us to sang (not sing, but sang). We were *excited!*

Being that my paternal grandmother had passed away, her sister stepped in and did what only a sister could; she filled the gap. She didn't have any kids of her own. She was our babysitter while our parents worked. Truth be told, we hung out at her house even if our parents were off. Her house was like our second home. It was a second home to a lot of the neighborhood kids as well.

Her porch reminded me of the wooden floors in our church. Not only was it our safe place, but all of the kids would have full-blown church services on her porch. Everybody knew their role in our pretend church service. We had a pastor, a choir director, a deacon, and even members of the congregation. We would be clapping and singing as somebody pretended to preach their hearts out. *We had church.* We dressed up in curtains or whatever we could get our hands on, no matter the consequences. We had a vivid imagination for sure. We would sing old hymns as if we had certainly experienced life while stomping our feet on the wooden porch. In actuality, we didn't have a care in the world.

We had no idea what the songs meant, but you couldn't tell us that we did not have an encounter with God! We were such great actors (or maybe not). Looking back, I wonder whose idea it was. Like did somebody just say, "Hey, you guys, let's play church?" It kind of just happened. For some reason, we would all end up crying during the kid's church service on that porch, as if the Holy Spirit had fallen on us! We cried real tears. The "preacher" would use our personal experiences in his sermon. He would say something like, "Sheila, I know you fell off your bike today, but GOD is going to fix it!" and the amen corner would cheer him on as he dug deeper. But no worries, we had Ushers that would rub your back and fan you with whatever they got their hands on if needed. The weird thing is, we attended a Baptist church, so there wasn't a lot of falling out or crying. But during our porch church service, we incorporated it for sure.

My great auntie was the master of baking cakes. She had the best cakes in Milledgeville if you ask me. Besides keeping kids, she sold cakes and did hair for a living. Eventually, she would come out and run us off by yelling "Ya'll are going to make my cakes fall with all this stomping," or "Ya'll gonna stop playing with God after a while when he gets a hold of ya!" We had no intentions of playing with God, but I think he got a hold of a few people on that porch. Auntie was a Jill of many trades. She also washed clothes for a lady by the name of Mrs. Jewel. After all of her hard work, we would go through those freshly washed clothes and find things to dress up in. We would find curtains or towels to tie around us. It didn't matter what it was; we made it work. Well, at least we made it work until my auntie discovered what we were doing. When that happened, she would simply say, "WAIT ONE MINUTE!" That was all she had to say. We were all familiar with those three words, and we knew to scatter at that point because she was headed to get a switch. It was not just any switch, her switches stood upright by themselves. We knew how to get out of those clothes faster than she could say those three words.

She believed in spanking, and when that didn't work, she had a backup plan for the boys. My dad didn't believe in spankings, and I believe this is why I was spared. But if you ask me, it was because I was a very sweet child (inserts laughter). There was one time that she came through that porch spanking everything in sight, and I caught the end of the switch and she immediately stopped and apologized. I deserved the hit. I know I did. I kind of considered it an honor to be included with the others. My favorite cousin, of all people, felt that I deserved it as well. She never let me or my auntie live that down. She would continuously ask, "But why did you have to apologize to Sheila?" Or "She-She" as my auntie would call me. She demanded answers, but Auntie would pay her no mind. She actually threatened to hit her again if she kept asking. She asked this well into our adulthood.

Auntie Mamie was a godly woman, but just know, that she could use a few choice words and she didn't mind pulling out her pistol if she needed to! She would even fire a round in the air if those boys got out of hand. But she always gave her infamous warning so that anyone in her path could clear the way. WAIT ONE MINUTE! That was the warning that we all knew very well. They knew not to play with her. She would fire at least three shots in the air as we all covered our ears. We knew when it was coming. Those boys would run off and stay gone for hours until she calmed down. The rest of us would sit there quietly, praying that she didn't actually shoot one of them. One night, I thought for sure she had killed one of them as it took him far too long to come back home. That woman loved us and would lay down her life for us at any given moment. We would typically laugh about it the next day, but she didn't think it was a laughing matter at all. She had her own way of loving us. She made everybody feel special. She was our very own Madea!

Auntie had one television in the house. There was so much love shared in that TV room while watching our favorite shows. There had to be ten kids crowded in that small room at any given time. All of whom were sweaty from playing outside all day. We made it work, though. Every now and then, a storm would come up, and we would be stuck in the room for longer than we anticipated. She was the first to teach us to sit down and be quiet during a storm. She would say, "Don't you hear that the Lord is working?" When she really meant business, she would call you by name multiple times as if you didn't hear her the first time. "She- She, *She-She*, SHE-SHE (The third time was always loudest); I need you to sit down now and let the Lord finish working, you hear me?"

"Yes ma am," I replied, as I rolled my eyes at whoever got me in trouble. So, we would gather around and sit still until we eventually fell asleep listening to her sing beautiful hymns. I swear I believe that she had a direct line of communication with God!

Once the storm let up, we headed back to the yard. We played everything from kickball, Simon Says, freeze tag, ring around the roses to hide-and-seek. We had hula hoop contests that lasted for hours. The girls made mud pies and collard greens out of leaves on a routine basis. The boys nailed old bicycle rims to the trees to play basketball. We kept ourselves busy until Auntie would call four of us in at a time to have dinner. We patiently waited our turn. The girls went first, followed by the boys. Auntie Mamie had an abundance of love to share, and we all felt it. She probably had the least to give in our family, but she always gave the most.

Now back to my favorite cousin (aka "Fav") and I singing the lead part in the church choir. We had practiced for months. We would sing it on Auntie Mamie's porch amongst a congregation of our peers. We would sing it in the car, in the tub, and everywhere we went. The time had come for us to sing it on Sunday morning at church. We had on our Sunday best. I can remember my floral dress that came with a flower to go in my hair. This was a plus because my coarse hair usually looked a mess, but my auntie did the best that she could with it before sticking that flower in it. The choir director motioned us to make our way to the microphone, the pianist began to play our song, and we knew it was show time. That was *our* song. This was our big moment. The two of us locked our eyes and took our position. We were ready! We had been preparing for this moment our entire lives it seemed. The choir began to sing, and our part was quickly approaching. I was supposed to go first as I'm the oldest. But we have always had each other's backs and stepped in wherever needed. The choir stopped singing, and the choir director pointed at me. Eager to start, I sang the first three words before something completely zapped my strength. Every muscle in my body froze. My jaws were locked. Thinking back, I don't even know if I could still see; I was just that nervous! I believe I temporarily lost my vision. I lost *the* vision, for sure. The vision that we had painted I didn't see a soul in that church. I couldn't even see myself.

The choir resumed the chorus portion of the song to stand in the gap, and they circled back to Fav for her part. The choir director pointed at her more firmly as if to say, don't you mess up! I knew she was going to bring it on home because we had practiced, and she always picked up my slack. Just as I had, she started out strong with the first three words. The very same force that had taken over my body must have jumped onto her because, my golly, she was stuck, too! I couldn't look at her. I refused! I couldn't face her. Besides, I can't even remember if I could see at the time. Once again, the chorus resumed their portion of the song. We returned to our seats, refusing to look at each other, any of our cousins, or her mom, who was sitting on the second row in the congregation. We looked straight ahead at the exit and contemplated our escape.

After church, we made what seemed to be the longest journey to my aunt s minivan in the parking lot. I would have given anything to be able to walk home that day, and we lived about fifteen miles away. Although my auntie and I joke all the time now, back then, she and my dad had a very serious demeanor. They weren't mean, just serious. There was no joking! We loaded into the van, and she did not say one mumbling word! *Not one!* But leave it to my older male cousin. After a long awkward silence, he blurted out, "I got something to say." Like my dad, he always stretched his words to make them much longer than they were. He turned to look at me and Fav and said "Why," he drew out, "Just *why* did y'all get up there and embarrass the WHOLE family?" Y'all didn't just embarrass yourselves, y'all embarrassed the whole family's name!" He ridiculed us the entire ride home. Nobody stopped him. No one came to our rescue. He went on and on. It's hilarious now when I think back on it, but at that time, we hung our heads in despair.

Fav mustered up the coverage to tell her brother to shut up, but I didn't even have the strength to do that. I wanted to cry out, "It's me, Lord. Come save me, I need You!" Instead, we sat there quietly and waited for the storm to pass.

Chapter 7:

A Broken Heart

After spending the summer chasing my best friends, balls, and fireflies, the time had arrived for me to step into high school. My nerves gripped me tightly. I was excited but nervous. It wasn't a good look if the upperclassmen could tell that you were scared, so I smiled and put my best foot forward as I entered the humongous new school. It was twice the size of my middle school. I felt like the kid who climbed onto the bike that was twice her size. This time, I was eager to conquer the task at hand.

If I was ever a know-it-all, I was surely one once I entered high school. This must have been what Auntie Mamie meant when she would say that someone was smelling themselves. She never meant it in the natural sense. In addition to the things that she did to make a living, she also sold cosmetics, fragrances, skincare, etc. She always made sure that we had the latest oils and deodorants. She didn't mind telling you if you smelled "rank" after a game of kickball. She kept it real. If she ever told you that you were smelling yourself, it had nothing to do with your scent. It had everything to do with your prideful attitude and the need for you to humble yourself.

I was still that little girl called Boot in JB s eyes, even as a high school student. He would still greet my sister and I at the door before school to make sure that our faces were shiny as he pulled his used peppermint ChapStick from his pockets and spread it well beyond the outline of our lips. I've never had small lips, but he could never seem to stay within the outline of my lips. Dry lips were certainly a pet peeve of his. This routine continued for long as I could remember. Not only did he greet us to wish us well for the day, but he would also give me a lecture on how I needed to sit down, keep my mouth shut and listen while I was at school. Every one of my teachers had consistently reported that I talked too much during class since the time that I was in Pre-K. He would say, "Those teachers got theirs; sit down and listen so that you can get yours." I guess he was referencing an education. My dad would wrap up his morning routine by telling me to smile. It was important to him that I smiled with my freshly greased lips. He would always say, "You're too pretty not to smile. Fix your face!" He would remind me of this often, so if nothing else, I knew how to smile, even if I didn't feel like it. This aligned with what my mom taught me as well. Her motto was if you look good, you feel good! She would say that once the door to your home opens, you should look your very best, no matter what you face beforehand. So, if nothing else, I learned to smile and look my best!

I wasn't a bad kid, or at least I didn't think so. But my demeanor did change in ninth grade. For one, I began dating. I know what you are thinking, and I agree. Looking back, it was way too early to date! But that's when I started. My "friend" would call, and my dad would politely hang up the phone in his face. He would act as if he couldn't hear anyone on the other end of the line. Or he would yell, "Who is this calling here? He sounds as old as me." I assure you that he didn't have a deep voice at all, and he was a junior in high school and nowhere as old as my dad. I don't even know if it was technically considered dating because I couldn't go on an actual date. Nor could he come and visit me. That was a given and completely out of the question. Nevertheless, that s what we called it.

I've always done what I needed to do in school, other than talking too much. Well, maybe not. With dating came trouble! I did get into a couple of fights. Now, if my dad were telling this story, he would say that I got into a lot of fights. One fight was too many for him!

One fight in particular stands out to me. The day started no different than the other days. He met me at the door, told me to behave and listen to my teacher, and he made sure that I had his peppermint ChapStick smeared outside the borders of my lips. I don't even recall what the fight was about, but I remember sitting in the principal's office waiting for my dad to arrive afterward. I hung my head in shame and prepared my pouting spill to explain to him my reasoning.

The principals all knew him well due to a prior incident where he had to give them all a piece of his mind, but that's another story. He didn't mind doing that. When I was much older, he explained to me that a kid stole his shoes when he was in school. My dad demanded that the kid give him back his shoes. The principal called his dad into the office. He explained that he felt that things would be okay once his dad arrived and could vouch that the shoes belonged to him. To his amazement, no such thing happened. As he put it, his dad responded "yes sir" to everything the principal asked and never defended him. They left the office without the shoes that belonged to him. Because of that incident, he was determined to hear his child's side of the story and stand his ground. It was astonishing how that stuck with him all those years. Now, I am sure that he grew up in a time when his dad's life was on the line had he responded in any other manner. His dad bought him another pair of shoes, but it still tarnished his pride. He knew that I wasn't always right. As a matter of fact, I wasn't right half of the time, but I always knew that he had my back, even if that meant that we would talk about my wrongs a little later.

This time, when my dad walked into the principal's office, the energy was different. He wasn't giving me a loud lecture as he was known to do when I was in trouble, which kind of scared me because I was prepared. I had rehearsed my explanation a thousand times over in my head. I m sure the principals were prepared to answer all of his questions as well, but he had none. My dad never laid hands on me in the form of punishment, not even once. As you can imagine, there were times that even I felt it was warranted. His lectures were his discipline. He didn't allow anyone else to physically discipline me either. But on that day, he simply said, "You gotta keep your hands off these folks; stay away from them if you can't get along!" I climbed into the cougar, and we went home with the oldies blaring in our ears. This was unreal, and I wondered if he was okay. Was he sick? Did he finally see my point of view that sometimes fighting was necessary? I needed him to say something! Say anything! Maybe he was trying to show me that in some things you cannot fight physically.

Shortly after we got home, he came into my room and sat on my bed. In my mind, I thought, "Here we go," but I was prepared to tell him that it was someone else's fault. He *absolutely* hated when I would place the blame on someone else.

He was quick to say, "I am not their dad, and I don't want to talk about them and what they are doing." That didn't help my storyline at all. But instead, he said, "My dad died, and I need to go out of town."

I didn't have a speech planned for this, and I scrambled for words. I didn't know what to say! I didn't know how to feel. He didn't cry. At this point in my life, I had only seen this giant shed one tear: just one! And that was at my maternal grandmother's funeral. But even then, he quickly dried that one tear and continued comforting me.

So, we sat there on the edge of my bed in silence. He wasn't a very affectionate person back then, like a hugger or anything. He showed his love with every ounce of his being. It just wasn't shown via affection. He was a provider. He showed his love with gifts. He not only gave us what we wanted but everything that we even thought we wanted. I wanted to hug him and tell him how sorry I felt. I was disappointed in myself, to say the least. I had let my dad down in a major way on a major day! I had no words, so the silence grew louder.

I only met my grandfather once that I can remember. He lived in Detroit, and we lived in Georgia. But I do remember the day we met. I was five years old. I remember him asking how old I was and giving me five dollars because of my age. My dad would do that, too, back then. When I turned six, I got six dollars, so forth, and so on. Even then, I thought I would have to be old and gray to strike it rich at that rate. My dad was excited to introduce us even as a kid, I could tell! But then again, my dad got excited when he introduced his kids to anybody.

JB prepared for his trip to Detroit for the funeral, and I stayed home and waddled in disgust! Why couldn't I just go to school and shut up? A girl my age had no business getting into fights. I really beat myself up about it. I don't think that a spanking could have punished me more than I punished myself. He needed me that day and I was fighting about something that I can't even recall today. There were no excuses. After my suspension was over, I returned to school.

I'm not sure why it was so hard to be quiet; I guess I always had something to say. I had things on my mind that needed to be voiced. But considering the fact that I wanted to be a teacher, you'd think I would have been more attentive. I practiced being a teacher for years at my Auntie Mamie s house. Just like we had church service, we had class. When class was in session, it was serious business. JB had even bought me a bright red chalkboard in my younger years to support the vision. I would write messages to him on that chalkboard for him to find them later. "Sheila loves her dad forever!" was plastered on the chalkboard on a regular basis. My goals changed some time later.

My dad suffered a *heart attack during my freshman year of high school!* Although I was only fourteen years old, this shifted my life. My soldier, the strongest person I knew, suffered a heart attack. Of course, I didn't know much about a heart attack or what it entailed at the time. He was hospitalized in a neighboring city at a larger hospital in Macon, Georgia, so I wasn't allowed to see him for a couple of days. That was the longest two days of my life.

One of my aunts finally came to pick me up to take me for a visit. I wanted to see what all the fuss was about. I had never been away from my dad for too long, and I had certainly never seen him in a weakened state. An hour-long trip seemed to have taken eight hours at least. We eventually arrived at the hospital. As the door to his hospital room swung open, the hospital bed was in clear view. He was lying there, and he was way too still, in my opinion. There were too many tubes attached to him. Too many machines making noises and I couldn't figure out why. My thoughts could not catch up with what my eyes were seeing. I hadn't talked to God in a while but wondered if he remembered my prayer. Surely, he hadn't forgotten, besides he s God.

I froze in my tracks momentarily before puking my guts out. All my emotions exploded through my stomach, and I vomited right there in the hospital room! I wanted my giant to get out of that bed. I wanted to know what the tubes were! I wanted to know what the meds were! I wanted to know why total strangers were touching him. I wanted him to look at me and tell me that everything was going to be ok. I even wanted him to call me Boot! Earth Angel plunged towards me to usher me out of the room. Once I was all cleaned up, she attempted to prepare me to go in and see him again. I had far too many questions. I knew at that very moment that no matter how long it took, I was going to figure it out for my JB. And if that meant becoming a nurse, then a nurse I would be! I don't recall revisiting the hospital during that admission, and I'm sure I blew it by vomiting! But I knew that my giant would rise out of that bed. I was staying with my mom, and I m sure I drove her crazy asking questions she didn't have answers to. We didn't have cell phones just yet. I had a beeper, but that wouldn't help me check on his progress.

A few days later (against doctor's orders), JB pulled up in that cougar and blew the horn, a horn I was familiar with. The sound of that horn made me rise to my feet instantly. It was the number one signal that my daddy was there. Sure enough, it was him, and I was excited to hear, "Come on, let's go, Boot." At that point, I didn't care if he was affectionate. Not knowing his pain level, I gave him a big hug. He made a very slight facial grimace. But other than that, he looked at me as if nothing had ever happened while returning the tight hug. He had a way of doing that. The look was sort of like a "what are you looking at" kind of deal. So, I quickly turned away, not wanting to stare, and that s exactly what he wanted. The king of lectures rarely ever addressed the elephant in the room when it came to him! The incision on his chest was evident through the muscle shirt that he was wearing. He was straight out of the hospital and had already resorted to his muscle shirts. He refused to show any signs of weakness!

I still didn't fully grasp the concept of what a heart attack actually meant. I remember thinking, how could someone with such a big heart have a broken heart? So, I quickly exhaled a sigh of relief that he was ok, climbed into the cougar, and drove off into the sunset as we had done so many times before. In my eyes, things were back to normal. He turned the music up as loud as it could possibly go, blasting the good ole oldies. At that moment, I was reminded that God had not forgotten how much I needed JB and all was well in my world as I drifted off to sleep while listening to something along the lines of "How Can You Mend a Broken Heart" by Al Green.

It's Only a Test

Those sweet high school years seemed to fly by. Immediately following my father s heart attack, I sprang into action and began taking courses to learn more about healthcare. I don't think I ever outgrew talking so much in school, though. Again, I had stuff I needed to say, and it always seemed to be at the most inopportune time. I became a certified nursing assistant before graduating high school. And although that was a short-term goal to lead to a nursing degree, my dad celebrated it as if I had graduated from medical school. He always celebrated the small wins. He had a way of making you feel like no one in the world could do it like you could, no matter what the "it" was.

He would say, "You did it, Boot," while sliding a monetary reward into my hand.

He started encouraging my shenanigans early in life. For instance, he would spend what seemed like hours shopping for a birthday card for others. When I was younger, I wanted to scream, "Dude, just pick out a card already!" Just when I was certain that he found the right one, he would politely place it back on the shelf. He had to ensure that the card said everything he wanted to say to that person. He was a brutally honest person, so if it didn't sound like him, he wasn't interested in purchasing it. It obviously was very difficult to find something that fell into that category. He was a man who meant what he said and said what he meant.

Anytime I gave him a card, whether it was homemade or purchased, he encouraged me to read it aloud with a little twist. When I finished reciting it, he would ask, "Do you really mean what you said or is that just what the card says?" We had this thing where it was a full-blown performance when I read him his card. It s a wonder that I wasn't an actress the way he encouraged my shenanigans. He was quite the actor too because he would act as if I deserved an award for the presentation itself. This continued throughout my adulthood. I honestly don't ever remember giving him a card that I didn't have to act out.

I learned that my capabilities were endless at home. They built my esteem for sure. He trusted me and my abilities, even with money! I can remember us taking a family trip to the bank my sophomore year, and moments later, I walked out with my savings account booklet in my hand. The way they ensured the banker included me in the conversation was impressive. It empowered me with a sense of belonging at the table. I probably walked into the bank with twenty dollars to my name not knowing what was about to transpire. By the time we left out of the bank I had access to nearly two thousand dollars deposited into my account. They obviously trusted me more than I trusted myself with money... Today, that may not be much money to some people, but this was a big deal in our household!

On one hand, I felt honored and on another hand, I felt like I was being pranked. As we pulled off to leave the bank, I thought, this has to be a test! Or maybe it's a setup! Either way, I was determined to pass it! I wasn't going to touch that money. There were times that I would use a few dollars, but I would be on edge until I replaced it. I wanted every penny to be accounted for if, by some chance, he checked my account. This instilled the value of saving within in It also instilled a principle that I still, to this day, believe. That at any given moment, I should at least have what my daddy gave me! It doesn't always happen, but yet it s the goal.

I'm not sure if he ever checked the account or not. He believed that you should always have some money in your pockets when leaving the house. When I would get ready to leave, he would say something like, "You got some money, don't you?" while slipping some into my hand as if I answered no. He trusted me way too much if you asked me. He also knew that I would come to him if I needed him, sometimes too often.

I know that I have credited my dad a lot. Besides, the book is about our relationship, but he truly had a gem by his side. By this time, I had learned to appreciate her for the angel that she is. My sister and I were probably known as those girls who were spoiled by their dad (which we were). However, Earth Angel is the type of person who blesses you and hides her hand. She went above and beyond for our entire family. I m certain that the bank trip was her idea. She always allows others to shine. My dad would not have been able to do a lot of the things he did without her.

I guess I passed the test. During my junior year of high school, he brought me my first car. It was a shiny red Dodge Neon sports coupe (his favorite color). I didn't even know how to drive at the time, so of course, I didn't have a license. But I had a car! If nothing else, I could look out that window and admire it, and that alone was driving me crazy. He purchased a car tag to place on the front of the car that read "fear this!" You read it right, fear this! Now I still don't understand what made him do that, but I didn't say a word about it. His cougar still had "Eddie s Love" on the sides and on the front tag read "Sheila & Sharris." That's my sister and me. He believed in adding a personal touch.

I was just as proud of my car as he was of his cougar. He had purchased brand new rims to go on it, and he always kept it washed. He used to say, if your car is dirty, then you might as well not take a bath. I never understood that concept, but hey, I appreciated the car wash, nevertheless.

It was then that I learned the peace that resides inside your own car. My dad would always spend time in his car listening to his music. Just sitting there staring into space. He didn't sing along. He simply appeared to get lost in his thoughts as he listened. He didn't dance at all! Every now and then he would tap his fingers on the steering wheel while the music played as loud as it possibly could. I continuously jumped into "fix it" mode when it came to my dad; so often I would interrupt. In my mind, he must have had a lot on his mind for him to be in such deep thought. So, I would tap on the window and say something stupid like can you take me to the store, just so we could go for a ride. Now surely this would add to his stressors if anything, but in my mind, I was distracting him from the cares of this world. Once I got my car, I realized the peace that resides inside your car; with just you and your music!

My senior year was full of fond memories. For my senior prom, I wore his favorite color, a beautiful red dress. Our theme was "A Night to Remember," and it was nothing short of that. I was just beginning to loosen up and dance a little bit. I couldn't dance a lick then, and it s no better today. One of my close friends walked up to me while I was on the dance floor making a fool of myself. She let me know that my dad was *inside* of the prom. How did that happen, I wondered? Who allowed my dad into the prom? Surely it had to be a mistake. Her eyesight had to be playing tricks on her. Nope! Surely enough, there he stood in his suit with a matching red blazer to match my red dress! Earth Angel was dressed in her Sunday best. They even had my sister dressed as if she was staying for the remainder of the prom. I quickly rushed over and gave him a "How can I help you?" look. You know the kind that he typically gave when he didn't want someone looking at him.

Obviously, he had no idea what this would do to my reputation as a senior in high school. But by the look on his face, neither did he care! He wanted a full photoshoot and I obliged so that they could quickly get going. If I could turn back the hands of time, I would have danced the night away with those who meant the most to me. Our little family bubble was a safe place!

Despite being the motor mouth in class, I managed to graduate as scheduled in 1997. I had big dreams of attending a big college as far away from home as possible. However, my dad politely said, "We have colleges right here at home," as if going away was the craziest thing he had ever heard. So that's exactly what I did. I started school right there in my hometown. Things were looking up. I desperately wanted to make him proud. I was growing up and off to become a nurse! Or so I thought.

Chapter 9

There s Nothing Left to Say

I enjoyed that summer after graduating high school. I spent a lot of time with family and friends and simply rode around town in that red Dodge Neon with "Fear This" on the front. Dear God, why did I have that on the front of my car? Because my daddy thought that you should "Fear This," that's why. But yes, I enjoyed that summer. I had somehow picked up the tradition of riding around town with no particular place to go. My Earth Angel stayed on me about college. She made sure that I was enrolled in time. She filled out the applications, financial aid paperwork, and all. She was serious about school.

I started college as scheduled that August after graduating in May. I didn't enjoy it as much as I thought I would. Not the core classes, at least. Remember, I was a know-it-all and couldn't understand why I still needed to take Math and English classes. I just knew that I would be done with all of that after high school. I wanted to be a nurse. I wanted someone to teach me why my dad had a heart attack. I did not want to learn fancy math or how to write papers. I wanted to get to the juicy stuff. The worst part of all, they had me taking art. Art! Yes, *art!* Of all things, an art class. I was no artist. It was one of the hardest classes I have ever taken! I wonder if my Earth Angel had anything to do with that? She must have filled out the paperwork incorrectly because this had to be someone's fault other than my own. Who in the world registered me for an art class I thought to myself every time I entered the classroom. I would get sick as soon as I walked into class, physically ill. I didn't want to be there. I would go to sleep two minutes into the lecture. Thinking back, that was extremely disrespectful. I literally had no interest in the subject at all. It wasn't much later that I determined that I was sick in all of my classes. Maybe this school thing wasn't for me. It was beginning to affect my health. I wanted to be able to take care of others but at this rate, I needed someone to take care of me.

Once the nausea became debilitating and I do mean debilitating, I decided that I needed to see a doctor. I wanted to explain to him how school was stressing me out and making me sick.

Maybe I was experiencing an allergic reaction to school and needed a doctor's excuse. The doctor had no such news.

He looked me in the eyes and said two words that temporarily deafened me. "You're pregnant," he said. I was fresh out of high school and in my very first semester of college and I was pregnant. How did this happen (well, not literally)? I obviously didn't spend that summer chasing fireflies. Why did this happen? Would I be able to finish school? How would I tell my parents?

I was flooded with questions that I didn't have the answers to. I was disappointed in myself yet again. I failed the test. The test that society had placed on me. I would become a statistic in the eyes of the world. I would be nineteen by the time I delivered my baby. I was still a baby myself! I was extremely sick as if my body was rejecting carrying a child. I would have to go to the hospital every few days just to get fluids. It was a while before anyone could tell that I was pregnant by the size of my belly because I literally could not hold down water. They probably thought I was dying. I was *sick*, but my parents knew. I never actually told them. I guess I learned that from JB. I could not address my own elephant. I remember puking my guts out one day and Earth Angel stood in the doorway of the bathroom with a look of disappointment all over her face. Of course, this wasn't her first time seeing me vomit, but this time she didn't rush over to assist me as she had done in the hospital. She just stood there and stared. She never told me that she was disappointed but her face said a thousand words.

I m not sure when my dad realized it but he stopped speaking to me. I mean, he completely stopped. No verbal exchange whatsoever! He would walk past me like I was a ghost! This broke me. He would not even turn his head in my direction for months. One day, me and my cousin were walking into the local shopping center, and he didn't even acknowledge me while in public. Now, that broke me on another level and caused my knees to buckle!

For some reason, my dad and I would always run into each other in the stores. He would greet me as if he hadn't seen me in years, turn and pay for all of my stuff. Any other time, Lord forbid if he saw someone he knew. He would introduce me like I was the president of the United States. He would let it be known that this was HIS daughter. Mind you, we lived in a small town and the person likely already knew me, but he didn't care. Not that time. He walked right past me and his head didn't budge. Now my dad never admitted to this incident as long as he lived, b. But I will never forget it. In later years, when I would bring it up, he would swear up and down that he never saw me. My cousin even spoke to him, but she was guilty by association, which meant she didn't get any love on that day either.

I told you earlier that my dad had a way with words. He could give a lecture to last you a lifetime, or he could cut your heart out with his words and hand it to you on a platter. As an adult, I m thankful he chose to remain quiet instead of saying something he could not erase. I was broken at the fact that he ignored me, but I had broken him. His baby was having a baby! I can't imagine what that did to him. I don't remember us reconciling during the pregnancy.

Earth Angel did what she could to keep the family together but the silent treatment was awkward. She would acknowledge the pregnancy by referring to the baby and me as y'all. She would try to cook anything that I could tolerate. She would say things like, "What do *y'all* want to eat?" I knew that they would go to the end of the earth for me, so I sat in the shame of hurting them! Again, I don't remember me and my dad reconciling before my delivery. He did eventually make eye contact to let me know that I wasn't a ghost, but he would not speak. He still didn't believe in dating; it didn't matter if I was pregnant or not.

The very first time the baby s father came to our house was to assemble the baby bed. I was still scared for him to come. My dad stood in the doorway and watched the entire time that he assembled that bed. I know that the "dad" in him wanted to step in and show us both how it should be done, but he didn't. I guess he decided that he had to release his grip in order for me to pedal. I would much rather someone talk to me, even if angry so I could at least know what they were thinking. We were so nervous. He was probably hoping that we would ask him to help us out. But he didn't say a word and neither did we. This is a toxic trait that I carry still to this day; I can pretend that people don't exist! Help Lord! He was emotionally broken, and I m sure that he felt at that time that there was nothing left to say. This was the first and the last time I've ever experienced this with my dad.

So, the time came for me to deliver my Destiny. I remember my dad walking into the delivery room in his basketball jersey and his jeans with extra starch applied to them. He walked over to my bed and grabbed my hand. I saw a tear fall from his eye. This was the second time I had witnessed a tear fall with this guy. This was the second and final time that I ever witnessed it. Both times, it was just one tear. He held my hand for what felt like an eternity! He didn't have a lecture prepared and the labor pains were coming back-to-back. He finally found his voice that had been missing toward me for months and whispered, "It will be over after a while, Boot."

After twelve hours of labor, I ended up undergoing surgery to deliver the baby and was unable to care for myself, let alone a baby, for the first couple of weeks. My Earth Angel stepped up to the challenge, though. God had shown me so many times before that she was the answer to so many of the prayers, although it took us some time to learn each other. Her heart was surely evident during this time. Not because of what she did for me or my child but just because of who she is. She loved me during a time in which I hadn't properly learned to love myself. I was a spoiled brat, but she toughed it out and loved the hell up out of me.

Babies are such a blessing, even if the timing isn't right in human eyes. Looking back, this baby softened my giant and built me up. He was a different man afterwards. He was gentle with her. He would poke her belly and she would laugh like there was no tomorrow. He didn't believe in tickling, so it was just a poke. This was evident when me and my sister were kids. He would immediately stop someone if they attempted to tickle either of us. So I guess the poke was his way around it. He made mud pies with this new kid! He never made mud pies with me! Once she began to walk, wherever he went, she went. The rides to the store now belonged to her. He now came home with her lollipops. He was just a different person overall. I saw him in a different light. He was now a *gentle* giant.

We moved into our own place shortly after I gave birth. I knew that this was an elephant that I would have to address with my dad. I practiced how I would tell him. I couldn't bear another "silent treatment," and I couldn't risk our relationship again. I knew this would be another dagger for him, but I wholeheartedly thought it was the right thing to do. I had never even been picked up for a date from my family home, and now I needed to tell him that I and the father of my child were getting our own place. It wasn't an easy task at all. I knew that I wanted to have a conversation with him. I contemplated writing him a note, which would not have been unusual for me. I wrote him letters all the time. But this was different. He was sitting on the couch in the living room; this was his favorite spot. I walked past him several times with every intention of breaking the news, but once I came close, I would speed walk right past him. Finally, I walked in, all prepared for my speech, and I crumbled, just as I had in the church choir. I opened my mouth and the only thing that came out was, "I m moving out. Can I take my T.V. with me?" I know, stupidest thing ever, but that s what I said (sigh)! Out of all the things I probably needed, I asked about a T.V. He stared at me as if I had lost my mind. He just looked at me for at least ten seconds. But it felt like ten years.

He responded, "Yeah." That s it. I had poured out my heart in my mind and he just said, "Yeah," and turned his attention back to the T.V. A few days later, he came into my room and had a seat. I knew this meant that it was lecture time. But he didn't lecture me at all. I told you that he was a different man. He asked for the details and asked if I was sure. I assured him that I was. To my surprise, he gave me a hug and left it at, "I love you."

Chapter 10:

Don't Ever Forget Me

I was an adult and doing things independently for once, just like the very first time JB turned the bicycle loose. I was still looking back to say, "Look, Daddy, I can do it!" even in my adult years. Raising a baby, going to school, and working full-time was rough, to say the least, but I had a lot of support! My army showed up for me, especially my Earth Angel. Destiny was "our baby." She would work nights and keep our baby while I went to school during the day. She was constantly offering encouragement and filling in the gaps where she could. I tried to do the adult thing and put my baby in daycare, but she wasn't having it. It was a waste of money because Earth Angel was picking her up an hour after arrival. My dad would even watch her if my Earth Angel was busy, but he didn't do diapers. The Lord forbid if she needed changing; he would take her to my aunt Mamie s house just so she could change the diaper, and off they would go.

My dad has always known that I had vivid dreams all of my life, so we would discuss them often. I would call him early in the morning, and he would say, "Did you have a crazy dream?" He thought this was why I was afraid of the dark. We would laugh about it, and he would reassure me that it was just a dream. I had begun working at the local nursing home utilizing that certificate I obtained in high school. Seeing dementia firsthand was kind of scary but those were my favorite patients. Many of my residents had forgotten their kids. I immediately went to my dad in disbelief and voiced my concerns about how it would destroy me if he ever forgot me. It became a nightmare that I feared would happen to me. Outside of his lectures, my dad was a man of few words. He looked me directly in the eyes and said, "I will never forget you!" Five simple words, but he said it with such authority, that I believed it to be true!

Chapter 11

Broken Glass

I eventually fulfilled my ninth-grade dream of becoming a nurse. Between my little sister and I, we gave our dad five grandkids that he absolutely adored. He didn't too much meddle in how we raised them, but we knew that if we needed to spank them it should not occur in his presence. He was a protector. He was also a giver. He enjoyed doing things for those around him. He had this saying, "Love is what it does" and he lived by that. Well into my adulthood, he would pick up my car every other week to ensure that it was detailed inside and out. Remember, he thought that if your car was dirty, you must be dirty too. This was a concept that I never grasped, regardless of my age. He had this thing where once he finished washing the car, he would circle the car several times to admire his work.

While I was working at the local hospital, each time he brought my car back to my job after cleaning it up, someone would always run up to me and say, "Someone is outside circling around your car," as if someone was trying to steal it.

Without even knowing that he had come to pick my car up, I would reply, "That s my dad." I knew it had to be him. The very next time he washed the car, someone different would come up and say the same thing. Eventually, everyone on the unit would say in unison, "That s her dad," and laugh about it.

He was diagnosed with hypertension as a young man. If he was admitted to the hospital, he grew to become all of our dad. Needless to say, he got a lot of attention from all the nurses. As a matter of fact, with my third pregnancy, one of my coworkers slipped up and told him that I was pregnant while she was taking care of him; not knowing that I hadn't told him yet. The co-worker only knew because I was so sick at work, and she would carry some of my load for me. Luckily, the thought of me carrying a child was not as traumatic for him as it was way back then. Earth Angel was a little salty that she found out that way, but she didn't hold it against me.

There were certain things that he only did for people he loved. He didn't wash cars for others because he put love into it. He would also manicure my lawn every Monday. That was another job he felt no one could do as well as he could. I couldn't agree more. He took pride in that grass. My Earth Angel would come along and manage the flower beds. She is known for giving people their flowers while they are living, instead of waiting until the funeral. Once he finished the lawn, he would admire it from afar; just as he did with the car. He would stay out there as long as it took until things were perfect in his eyes. My back door was a full glass door, and one day while he was cutting the grass, I heard a loud thump. I rushed over to the door with no concern at all for the door, but to make sure that my dad was okay. The glass was shattered. I wasn't worried because my JB left nothing undone, but I stood there in amazement looking at the glass. It didn't break all at once, but slowly broke into a million pieces. JB wasn't alarmed at all, disappointed but not alarmed. He promised to take care of it and resumed cutting the grass. The amazing part was the glass never collapsed. It was broken, yet still standing! JB had it repaired in no time.

Chapter 12

Small Town Girl

I loved growing up in a small town and had every intention of never leaving. By now I was married with three kids of my own. I would see friends who had previously moved away, and they would say, "Girl, you re still in the Ville?" We called it the "Ville," again, short for Milledgeville.

My reply would be, "I m never leaving as long as my dad is here," and I meant every word of it. I enjoyed having my village of family close by as well as my job. Life was good if you asked me, at least until I became complacent at my job. In a small town, there is only so far you can advance in your career without having to wait for someone to retire from a position or, Lord forbid, leave it for some unplanned reason. So, I started praying for guidance. If nothing else, I knew how to pray! *Dear God!*

Once I get a thought or goal in mind, it really begins to consume me. I mean, it lives rent-free in my mind all day long. I rest at night and awaken with the same thoughts the next day. I went to the source to explain how I was feeling. I poured my heart out to God, and he responded with one word. Just one! That word was, "Relocate!"

I went on to further explain to him, "Lord, maybe you didn't understand what I was asking for." I already had the plan sketched out and I wanted him to bless it. I wanted to work virtually from home, so I didn't think that relocating would be necessary, and besides my dad was still in this town.

I stressed that I wanted to work from my cozy home in Milledgeville with the repaired glass door. And he replied, "Relocate" as if I didn't hear him clearly the first time! I ignored it. Don't judge me, but I thought the master was confused. I continued to apply to work-from-home positions but nothing would happen! Nothing! I felt like I was hidden in plain sight. Absolutely nothing happened! I remember having this dream, yep, another dream, about me looking out the window onto the streets of the city. I have always loved to travel, so I thought nothing of it, but it continued to resurface in my thoughts. I also had a dream about walking through an unfamiliar house with my family. The house had a very specific design with multiple flights of stairs. Again, I thought nothing of it.

After applying for multiple jobs, I finally got a hit with a very large organization. I underwent the virtual interview, and I knew that I *nailed* it! Things were looking up for me! The only drawback was that I would have to fly out of state for training for eight weeks! Eight whole weeks! I did what I always do (other than pray) when I didn't know what to do; I called my Earth Angel. She was so excited! As always, she was explaining how she could help. She knew my overgrown tail was still scared of the dark, so we were trying to figure this thing out. She was already planning out how she and the kids could fly out to see me every other weekend, and I would come home the alternate weekend. I was worried about it being so far away and having to put that strain on her with the holidays coming up. What if my family couldn't get to me fast enough? Once we hung up, she sent me a text that has remained with me until this day. She expressed how much she loved me and that I would never be too far away for her to reach me. She is the humblest person that I have ever met, yet she was too stoic to voice it. I think it's because she didn't want me to hear her voice crack.

If I wasn't empowered already, I was certainly empowered after receiving that message from her. I was offered the job and accepted the position, and we began planning. The following day, I got a call from the recruiter to state that this enormous company had begun an unexpected hiring freeze!

I was shattered, just like that glass door, I couldn't figure out how I was still standing. The upcoming Sunday, the message at church was "God Blocked It" and the entire sermon slapped me all upside my head. It was like God was saying, "Maybe you didn't understand what I said; I said, *relocate!* I didn't ask you to temporarily go to training and return!"

I was left with a "geez" look on my face as I thought, "A whole freeze though, God? Is that what we are doing?"

I didn't tell a soul but I started applying for jobs in Atlanta. I wasn't even sure that I could drive in the city. The traffic was horrendous, and I still hadn't found where I lost my patience. I mean, I had driven in Atlanta, but not on a daily basis! Most of the time, I was asleep on the passenger side, while Jay (my husband at the time) did most of the driving. JB created a passenger princess many moons ago so there was no need in changing it now. And to be honest, I never had any intentions of changing my position to the driver seat.

I eventually got an interview and didn't even know how I would get there, but I knew who would have the answer! My Earth Angel drove me to the interview. She didn't ask any questions about the plan. We just went. Who does that? Who goes to an interview in a city, while not even sure if they are ready for the city traffic? I had been to ATL hundreds of thousands of times, but I don't recall visiting this particular street, yet the buildings looked so familiar. When around my parents, I always felt stronger than I really was. I never wanted to let them down, even if somehow, I let myself down. We didn't tell my dad that I had an interview, especially after the fiasco that the previous company pulled. He would get angry when my sister and I were upset about anything. He would say things like, "What's wrong with those folks?"

As if they should know that they needed to hire me! He would try to compensate for the hurt that someone else caused, usually by buying me something new and shiny, no wonder my love language includes gifts.

We marched into the huge building and signed in. Security only let Earth Angel so far before asking her to wait in the lobby. This reminded me of when JB had to release the bike and allow me to ride solo. She watched me with a look of "You got this" as the security guard escorted me to the interview. I felt like I did well in the interview. I knew that I had given it my best shot, but I didn't dare get my hopes up again! I didn't have a plan. I hadn't even explored the what-ifs. Like, where would I stay? That s important, right? It s like I was on autopilot, or more so like I was in the passenger seat as someone else drove. Someone other than Earth Angel.

As soon as we got home after the two-hour drive, I got a call offering me the job. Again, I didn't have a plan, but somehow, when I opened my mouth, the words, "Yes, I'll take it" came out. They wanted me to start in a little over two weeks. I didn't know what I was going to do, but I said *yes!*

I gave my Earth Angel a few minutes to make it back to their house, and I called her with the exciting news. Her response let me know that she wasn't surprised at all. She was confident that I would get the job all along. She calmly asked, "When do you plan to tell your dad?"

The world stood still. Now, I didn't have a plan about where I would live, but more importantly, who was going to tell my dad? I shrank to that little girl who asked him if I could take my T.V. with me because I had no other words. I responded, "Oh, I thought that you would tell him!"

And, of course, she said, "Absolutely not!" She even had the nerve to say, "Do you want me to put him on the phone?"

No, I thought. Why would I want her to do something as crazy as that? I needed to gather my thoughts! This was happening too fast! I couldn't figure out why we had not come up with a plan on the drive home. I needed input and she wasn't offering any! So, just like the time that I prepared to tell him that I was moving out, and similar to when my cousin and I practiced for our church song, I practiced what I would tell him! I went into full-blown rehearsal mode. I mean, I really practiced!

All I can remember was him answering the phone and saying hello—I know you didn't think that I would do it in person! Yep, I called him. I said, "Hey Dack." No longer "Jack" thanks to my little sister. She combined the words, Jack and Dad, so his new name was Dack! After those two words, my part of the conversation was inaudible! I mean, inaudible!

He must have thought I was having an emergency. He kept saying, "Say what now? Why are you crying? Stop crying so that I can hear you." It was apparent that he was getting upset.

I was saying, "I...I....I...got a job!" It was so bad that I couldn't catch my breath. Surely, this man had to think that I had lost my mind.

After a few minutes of trying to calm me down (probably while putting his shoes on to come over), he asked, "So you are crying because you are moving?" Remember, I did not even have a place to move to and it was only two hours away. He said, "This is why we sent you to school, so that you could make progress! You shouldn't be crying."

The whole world lifted off my shoulders in a matter of seconds. It was like he released the seat of my bicycle for the hundredth time, but this time, I was confident that I was ready! He was at my door less than fifteen minutes later.

Over the next week or so, I was pressed for time. I had to get busy and fast. We immediately connected with a realtor. We made the trip to the city to explore our options. It was an exhausting day of looking at rental properties that did not spark my interest. Yes, I had the audacity to turn down houses, knowing that I was about to be homeless. Well, not homeless. I still owned my home in Milledgeville, but I needed to move and do it quickly! I was discouraged and preparing to head back to my hometown with a feeling of defeat. My big brother stayed in the area, and I knew if push came to shove, I would invite myself to his house until I found a place.

Just as we were leaving, the realtor said, "Well, I could show you this house that is not listed yet."

Why not, I thought to myself, trying not to get my hopes up. She was very transparent that she didn't know when the house would be listed, and because of the school district, there would likely be a waiting list. Immediately upon entering the door, I knew that I had seen the house before. I whispered to Jay, "I dreamed about this house." We didn't talk about stuff like that out loud, because remember, I'm from Milledgeville, Georgia, and we were known to have one of the largest psych facilities in Georgia, if not the largest in the country. So, I whispered in hopes that the realtor wouldn't hear me. I didn't want her to think I had lost my mind.

Jay already knew I had lost my mind, but he supported the vision, nevertheless. He asked if I was sure. Of course, I was sure. At that point, she must have heard him because she stressed that the house was not listed yet and that it was a process!

She went on to explain that it was in a sought-after school district, and they don't last long. She also stressed that once it was listed, we would have to go through the application process, and so forth and so on. In other words, she was screaming that we may want to consider one of the other homes that she had shown. But I was sure. I knew the layout of the home before we toured it. It had three levels, much different from the ranch style I owned back home. In my dream, I kept going through doors to another level. Even in the dream, I wondered what we were doing in the house. As weird as it seems, I can sometimes talk to myself in my dreams. Or I ponder on it after I wake up. I would say things like, "Whose house is this?" "Why am I here?" Weird right?

Needless to say, we got the house. We moved into that non-listed house within the next couple of weeks. Not only that, but when I started my new job, my view from my office window was the city view that I had previously dreamed about. I knew those buildings looked familiar on the day of the interview. But once I made it to my office on the first day, I could then piece the puzzle together.

I m not psychic by any means, and the majority of the time, the dreams don't make sense until after the fact. I can barely remember where I put my phone half of the time when it s in my hand, so I surely can't tell the future. And God probably knew that if I envisioned the lottery numbers beforehand, we would all be billionaires by now! I do vividly remember my dreams, however. So, while some may consider it déjà vu, I can remember the exact dream.

Oh, and by the way, after the first year of working on the new job, I was working from home. I don't know why it was God s will for me to relocate. He often takes me on the scenic route to reach the final destination. I may never know, but nevertheless, his will always works out much better than my own. Besides, I learned while riding with JB, that it wasn't about the destination as much as it was the journey. I do know that things were finally looking up. No matter where my feet land, I will always be that small town girl at heart.

Who's Report Will You Believe?

The transition to the new town/job was seamless for the most part. My little family and I settled into our new home. It was different at first not having my "village" in the same town, but we quickly adjusted. Besides, we made sure that we had a guest bedroom so that they could visit as much as they would like.

I knew that although I worked in the city, I wanted to stay in the suburbs. The suburbs had the country feel that I was used to back home. With that being said I had a little bit of a drive to work. Wow, look at that, the little girl who was afraid of the traffic choosing to commute further, but hey, in Atlanta it s a long drive just to cross the street, considering the traffic.

I've always prayed for my dad. Well, I've prayed for a lot of people but especially for my dad. For some reason, after I relocated, those talks with God would take place in my car on the way to work. While talking to God, a 1.5-hour drive would feel more like fifteen minutes. The time would pass by fast. Looking back, I devoted more time to God during those commutes than I had done in a while. It almost felt like the times I shared with my JB during our rides together as a child. Maybe it was because my current playlist somehow reflected his playlist that I dreaded as a kid. How was that possible? I didn't blast it as loud as he did though. But I would sing along word for word to those oldies from the sixties and seventies. Maybe somehow, it took me back to those childhood rides to show me just how meaningful they were after all. Maybe this was my safe place. I was riding listening to my father's favorite playlist, while having meaningful conversations with my spiritual father.

My dad had not had any serious health conditions since the heart attack he experienced while I was in high school. I mean he would have times when his blood pressure was too high, and he would be admitted for a few days etc., but nothing major. I went to school to become a nurse so that I could assist in his health, if possible, but his health was not textbook by any means, and any of his doctors would agree. Besides, what I had learned, or what I thought I knew, went out of the window when it came to my dad.

I worked closely with his doctor in the hospital before I relocated. Don't tell the other nurses, but I think that I was one of his favorites. He was one of the smartest doctors that I have ever known. Yet, he would call me and say things like, "I just don't know, I m going to send him to another specialist," while referring to my dad. The number of specialists continued to grow, and they all would be puzzled by the clinical picture.

I would try very hard not to use medical terminology when I attended his appointments. I felt that everyone should receive the best care possible, and that should not change because a family member was in the healthcare profession. It wouldn't take long for them to discover it somehow. When discussing his treatment plan, they would all explain how grim things looked on paper, but how it did not align with his demeanor.

My dad was a hero! A real-life hero! And no matter how bad things were, he would reassure you that he was fine. He was also a firecracker. Remember, I told you that his words were like a sword sometimes. His patience was nonexistent! I mean, it literally did not exist. Well, except for with his grandkids. He hated hospitals and doctor's offices. He would say, "They are just going to find something else negative to tell me." And sometimes he would get rowdy. Never violent just rowdy while yelling out something like, "Just let me go home!"

He meant what he said and said what he meant. His primary doctor knew how to handle him though, but the newer specialists, not so much. When he wasn't rowdy, he simply ignored their very existence and pretended not to hear them speaking. At times they feared that something was medically or maybe even mentally wrong with him! They would look us, but we knew that he heard every word they were saying. We would call his name just to prove to them that he wasn't mute, and sure enough, he would answer. But shortly thereafter, he would brush the medical professionals off again. I would tease him and say that the doctors were going to put him on some psychiatric meds if he kept this up. I look back and wonder what he was thinking in those moments, or was he simply quieting the noise while he talked to God? Surely, he had a lot to tell God, and from the looks of it God had a lot to tell him. If I could use my imagination, I'm sure God whispered, "Whose report will you believe?"

Chapter 14:

Prepare Me

My dad was now out of sight since we relocated so he was in my prayers even more than usual. He was only two hours away, and I didn't mind burning up that road to get to him. We talked on the phone more as well. He would call and say, "Hey, this is Jack!" As if I didn't know who he was. He said that every single time he called. Every time! *Lord, what I would give to hear those words today!* After he had introduced himself, he would pause and just sit there as if I had called him. I found that funny, but only with him. It is a major pet peeve when others do it, and I will quickly question if they just called me to just sit on the phone, but our relationship was different. JB could do no wrong in my eyes, and If I did anything wrong, he would correct me in private after the smoke cleared. No one else would ever know that! It was our little secret. But anyhoo, my prayers had shifted at this point in my life, and of course, I was not praying that we would die together. I now had kids that needed me just as much as I needed JB. I would pray that God restored his health. I would pray that God would prepare me for whenever the time came for his transition. I would pray that I was at his side, whenever God decided to call him home. I honestly thought it would be humanly impossible for me to be prepared to live in a world without JB, but I also realized that it is impossible for anyone to live forever on earth.

One night, I was home entertaining a group of friends when I got a call from my Earth Angel. She shared that he wasn't acting right. We discussed his vitals and she said that she would monitor him for a little bit longer and call me back if anything changed. I was glued to my phone, so whatever we were celebrating at the house was no longer a celebration. She called me back to say that he had an episode of incontinence. It was like the National Guard sounded every alarm in Georgia. At least, that is what it sounded like in my head. My hero would never urinate on himself! Remember, this is the guy who thinks that if you don't clean out your car, you must not bathe. I had tunnel vision. I needed a helicopter. I insisted that they go to the hospital, and I would meet them there. With a house full of guests, I was scrambling to throw what I could in a bag and hit the road. Luckily, a good friend of mine was able to stay behind and lock up the house for me. I had already alerted her after the first call from Earth Angel. She knew how I felt about my dad. Anyone who knows anything about me knows how I felt about my dad. We must have done 100 mph trying to get to the hospital. My only thought was, "Dear God, prepare me!"

Once we made it to the hospital, we still couldn't see him for a while. I swear, I feel that my Earth Angel has the patience of Job! I don't. I have the patience of my JB, which is none at all. So, I paced the floor; I paced some more and then some more. I asked how much longer before we could see him thirty times or more. And before you say that I should know better as a nurse, at that point, I was no longer a nurse; I was strictly JB s daughter!

After what seemed like an eternity, they allowed us in the back. The doctor met with us prior and confirmed our worst fears, that he suspected a *stroke!* Of course, like every doctor before him, he was concerned with the overall clinical picture, so he planned to transfer him to another major hospital in Atlanta. I panicked. For some reason, my mind went back to my fear of him forgetting who I was. I would not be able to handle that. JB, you promised me, I said to myself as I made my way to his room.

Once I laid eyes on him, I could tell he seemed a little groggy and somewhat confused. But he looked good, considering they suspected a stroke. The doctor did his assessment by asking him where he was, the date, etc. None of which he could answer. At this point, my heart was about to literally jump out of my chest. I struggled to keep the tears within my eyelids to no avail. I leaned over and interrupted the doctor and said, "What s my name?"

JB looked at me as if I were the one confused and strongly replied, "Sheila!" I don't know why I did it, but I needed to know if he had forgotten me. I needed to know immediately. I released a huge sigh of relief. In my eyes, he was back. That was all the confirmation I needed at the time for Nurse Sheila to get herself together and refocus. I was then ready for him to make the transfer.

None of us got a wink of sleep that night. My dad was transported to the new hospital by ambulance and we followed in the car. Once we got there, my Earth Angel would do her tradition of cleaning the already cleaned bathrooms, etc., because we knew that we would be there for a few days.

Speaking of bathrooms, my aunt would not allow us to use public restrooms as kids. Lord forbid if we asked to use a restroom at someone's house, we were going to find ourselves in big trouble. This prepared me for the long shifts as a nurse with no restroom breaks. But it also prepared me for nights like this, where we would wait until we were assigned a room and my Earth Angel had done the official cleaning before we all took a restroom break.

We all got settled because no one was going home. That s one thing about it; we bonded during the hospitalizations. It's a wonder the hospital staff didn't kick some of us out. At any given time, you would find Earth Angel, all five grandkids, and my sister and I in the room. Not to mention any other family members that were visiting. There always seemed to be enough room, or maybe in hindsight we just made it work. My sister and I would take a corner of the bed; this was my favorite spot. The grandkids would take the let-out sofa. Earth Angel would usually be on her feet, making sure that everyone else was comfortable until time for her to go to bed. Just when we thought we were comfortable in whatever spot we chose, it would be time to exchange our spot with someone else. It didn't matter where we were as long as we were in the room. There was so much love in that room. Some nurses expressed that they could tell just how much he was loved. We all loved that man. He taught us how to love by his example. He always showed up for us; it was the least we could do in return. We would pray, "Lord, do what only you can do and prepare us for your will!"

Over the next couple of days, JB seemed to be making progress. He was back! And of course, he had begun to say things to the doctor like, "Just let me go home," as if he didn't just have a stroke. He had resumed pretending that he did not hear the doctors, so it was difficult for them to access his mental capacity following the stroke.

A few days in, he began to have a setback. Something seemed off so we requested that the imaging be repeated. I wasn't prepared for the response. The doctor confirmed that he indeed had a second stroke. I think my blood stopped flowing at that moment. JB had begun to babble again, and he could not answer simple questions like what year it was.

Just as before, I leaned in and asked him my name. He looked me dead in the eyes (with that what-are-you-looking-at look all over again) and said, "Sheila."

The doctor immediately said, "Do that again! Which we did. He always emphasized it; he knew I would pass out if he forgot me. I mean, I would have literally laid on the floor and thrown a temper tantrum. Of course, if he was not able to voice my name after a stroke, that does not mean that he forgot me. However, I was relieved that he could answer to settle any doubt. He knew exactly what I needed in those moments.

In my eyes, this was a sign that he was back! Critical but back. His situation was a little bit different. I told you that he was never a textbook hospital patient. The medicines for the stroke were contraindicated because of his heart valves from the heart attack. In layman's terms, his brain was bleeding, so he needed meds to stop the bleeding, but he also needed meds to thin the blood to prevent another heart attack. Which do you choose, your brain or your heart?

The doctors would call me out to point out the grim details of his lab reports. They were stunned at the findings. His clinical picture predicted death! But GOD! This was what I asked for in the ninth grade, right? I wanted to understand his clinical picture in times like this. I wasn't as strong as I thought, or maybe I was stronger in the ninth grade than I was as an adult.

The doctor pulled me aside to say, "You must prepare your family."

I wanted to get rowdy like JB and scream out in that ICU, "NO HELL I DON'T!" But instead, I responded, "He s going to be fine!" My faith and science were in a raging war, and science seemed to be winning. I saw the same things that the doctors saw, but this was my JB, and my faith was all I had.

My thoughts were racing at the speed of light. My aunt and I had dinner on the hospital grounds on the night of the second stroke. She was determined to get me out of the hospital room. I remember her mouth moving, but I didn't hear a word. Not one word! Not only was my faith and science fighting, but I was also fighting for my sanity. Lord, please don't let me lose my mind, I thought. I couldn't imagine life without JB. Every time I looked over his tests/ lab work, I wondered if my prayers were reaching heaven.

I was always intrigued by the story of Hezekiah. Not only because God extended his life but also because God changed his mind about something. Hezekiah was able to block distractions and remind God of his good deeds (2 Kings 19:14-21). I began to pray a similar prayer. I would pray that if there was anything JB did that was pleasing in his sight to spare him. Now, I am not saying that JB was spared solely because of my prayers because he certainly had a village praying for him, but I did my part when it came to prayer. I would drive home to shower/eat, and talk to God during the ride. I mean, I would *really* talk to God. The least I could do was intercede for a man who had literally interceded for me all of my life. Against all odds, JB recovered from not one but two back-to-back strokes and was discharged, as I knew he would be.

There is an old saying that a cat has nine lives. Well JB had the cats beaten. He would have a few setbacks, but he always bounced back. One day, he couldn't gather his thoughts into complete a sentence. That's the frustrating thing about strokes; you know exactly what you want to say, but you can't get the words out. The very next day, he would have a full-blown conversation. Some days, he couldn't walk but the next day, he would beat you to the car. He was very unpredictable.

It was a vicious cycle; every time we saw a new doctor, we would prepare ourselves mentally for them to come back, only to say that things looked worse than they thought. I could understand why JB was getting rowdy! It was no fault of the doctors; they were truly doing all they could. On another hand, for JB, there is only so much bad news that a person can take. We bonded more as a family during each admission, but at the same time, a piece of our hearts was chiseled based on the doctor's report. Yet, we continued to do the only thing we knew to do, and that was to pray! Our Father...

It was a week or so before Christmas, and JB was admitted back into the hospital. We all settled in and found our spot in the room after my Earth Angel did her initial cleaning. Christmas was a big deal for my sister, JB, and me. It s our favorite holiday.

JB always gave his Christmas gifts out early around August. He was different like that! He wanted to make sure it wasn't late. He would give my sister and me a lump sum of money for us and enough to get the grandkids what they had on their list. He wasn't big on shopping. He wanted to make sure that everyone got what they wanted instead of what he wanted them to have. We would still wait until Christmas and shower him with gifts. Earth Angel would give out her gifts on Christmas Day as well. JB was the only one who was early. We weren't too concerned about it being the holiday this particular year because if JB was in that hospital by golly, that s where all of us would spend the holidays.

The hospital went the extra mile with Christmas carols, Santa visits, etc. I was really impressed. The doctors were planning to take JB for a heart catheter so they could take a look inside his heart. He had one every so often since his heart attack, but this time was scary because they advised us that his heart was functioning at only ten percent, which meant it was getting weaker. This was a huge blow. Remember, at this point, we were jugging a stroke (brain bleed), his heart (blood flow blocked), and trying to maintain his kidney function. We didn't know how many more blows we could withstand as a family, but if you asked JB, he would tell you that he was fine. Maybe he was speaking those things that were not as though they were, or maybe this was his way of silencing the noise.

I tend to get clingy when I m emotional. I think this is a trait my sister and I picked up from my dad. He wasn't clingy at all, but if he knew you were dealing with something emotionally, he would come and spend the day with you and not even mention the elephant in the room. There was one time that I was going through heartbreak, and I knew he was aware of it. He made his way over to cut the grass, although it wasn't his scheduled grass day. The grass was just his excuse. After he finished, he came into the house, and we sat together in silence. Typically, he would leave after cutting grass to rush home to shower. But this time, he sat still. No lectures, no, "I told you so," just silence. This silence was different from the silent treatment that he gave while I was pregnant. This silence absorbed any weight that I was carrying. When the night fell, he gave me a hug and said something that will remain with me as long as I live. He said, "If it was up to me, you wouldn't know what pain felt like." I had been holding up all day, but of course, at that point, I melted in his arms. It wasn't because I was sad but because he made my world better just by being in my corner. My sister is the same way. She will come and bring you a snack and sit in silence, but the burden is absorbed by her presence alone.

As we sat around in the hospital room waiting for him to go down for heart surgery, my clinginess began to kick in. We prayed with him as we always did. The rest of the family went to get food, and I climbed into the bed beside him. I asked him if he was scared. With his superhero face on, he said no with an "Of course not" expression.

In a desperate attempt to pour into him, I began to tell him how he was the strongest person that I had ever known and how much I loved him. I explained that it was ok if he was scared, and he chuckled. I told him I didn't know what I would do without him. I had said that plenty of times before, but he acted as if it was the first time he had heard it. His eyes widened and I knew it was lecture time. I wasn't prepared. I was too weak—weak as water— but he kept it short.

He grabbed my hand and said, "You've got to be able to go on. We all have to leave here one day, and I need you to be able to keep going!" I knew that if I responded, the knot that was currently in my throat would be in my eyes, I would be bawling, and my words would become inaudible once again. So, I looked away while still holding his hand and pretended that he never said it. As soon as they took him down for the procedure, I began to remind God of Hezekiah s prayer.

The doctors were planning to discharge him shortly after his procedure, and things were looking up. My daughter was planning to stay the night at the hospital so that our Earth Angel could return home to prepare things. We were all excited about the possibility of him going home the next day. I was also excited to see my daughter courageous enough to take on that responsibility. She had grown into a teenager. We always made sure that somebody stayed with him overnight. So everybody else packed up and headed home so that the two of them could get settled for the night. JB was back on his feet once again!

My phone rang at about three a.m. and before the first ring was completed, I was flat on my feet. I heard my daughter s nervous voice on the other end stating, "Momma, I don't want to scare you, but something is wrong with Dak Dak." The hospital was about 45 minutes away from me and two hours away from Earth Angel. I think I must have been doing 120 mph, and she must have been doing 150 mph. Thank God for protecting us and everyone else on the road that night. Once we got there, no one could really tell us anything other than that they were trying to stabilize him. It was another night of hurry up and wait. We couldn't see him initially, but they promised they would allow us in as soon as they could.

My daughter explained that a team of nurses rushed into his room while they were sleeping and began working on him without saying much. She explained that the entire time JB was looking at her as if nothing was wrong. He had a way of doing that. You would have had to know him to understand that he was probably more concerned that this was happening in front of her! He was very protective. Especially when it came to those grandkids.

She handled the situation like a professional. I saw a twinkle in her eye that night! She wanted to know his clinical picture. She wanted to know what was happening. She wanted to be prepared if he ever found himself in this situation again. It was the same twinkle that I had in the ninth grade. I am proud to say that today she is a Registered Nurse as well.

As we suspected, JB had experienced some abnormal heart rhythms which required them to shock him back to a normal pace. We went back as soon as we could and as usual, he had the look of "What s wrong with ya'll?" on his face. He was more concerned about his grandbaby. Go Figure. He wanted to know if the nurses scared her. Every one of those kids was special to him.

He did end up being discharged around Christmas Eve. It was like a Christmas Miracle. The holiday was very special for our family that year, we had received the best gift ever—the gift of life. JB s days were unpredictable. We enjoyed the good days, as we never knew what the next second held. He could go months without another hospitalization, and sometimes it would be only days in between. My Earth Angel was there for the course. She made every appointment and had countless nights in those tiny hospital rooms. She was a full-time caregiver. She ensured that he had three cooked meals a day while he was home. She is still an energizer bunny to this day.

JB was readmitted shortly afterward. This admission, he wasn't speaking much, and when he did, we could barely make out what he was saying. He was barely walking. I grabbed my overnight bag and headed over to the hospital to give my Earth Angel some relief. This admission stands out to me because it was the first time that I recall seeing the disgust in his eyes. I cannot imagine having my thoughts trapped inside my head and not being able to express myself. My JB was trapped, and it frustrated him, which in turn frustrated me.

My Earth Angel is a caretaker/giver by heart so she would usually have everything laid out for me when I stayed overnight. Remember, most people thought that my sister and I were spoiled by our dad, which we were, but she had a lot to do with it as well. JB and I settled in for the night. She already had the pull-out sofa chair made up for me to sleep in, newspapers for me to read and multiple snacks lined the window sill. JB and I would find something on T.V. that would soon be watching the both of us. Usually, it was some form of sports, which I knew nothing about. Even though he could not make out his words, he would get his point across, especially if he wanted to watch a game.

For some reason, I woke up in the middle of the night and began flipping through the channels. I thought I could finally watch something other than football! All of a sudden, he sat straight up in the bed and yelled, "Nell!" while looking straight at me with a puzzled look. Nell was his mother's name. I have always been told that I look a lot like her, but JB also promised me that he would never forget me, so I knew it wasn't a mistake. But it scared the you know what out of me. So, I jumped up to begin assessing him to ensure he wasn't in pain. He could still answer yes or no questions appropriately. Then I asked the infamous question, and he responded, "Sheila." I knew that he wanted to be buried by his mom someday, but it wasn't happening on my watch that night. So, I politely told Nell that if she was visiting, JB was in good hands. If I had actually seen anything out of the ordinary, I was jumping out of that window from the third floor, and JB would have been on his own, unfortunately. Luckily the rest of the night was uneventful.

The next morning, I was preparing to bathe him. If he had an ounce of strength in him, he would not allow his kids to bathe him. We could do anything else but bathe him. He didn't want the staff to do it either. I tried to preserve his dignity by keeping him covered, and I would keep talking during the process, which probably didn't help the matter at all. That has never changed; I'm still a talker. He couldn't look at me, and I could see the disgust in his eyes. I told him things like how it was an honor to be able to assist him, but he continued to look away in disgust. I can only imagine his thoughts or his conversations with his Creator at that time. But I kept washing and drying as quickly as possible to restore his dignity. I had him all shiny with his lotion and smell goods. He loved to smell good and kept the latest colognes. Once we were done, he mustered up the strength to say, "Thank You." I reassured him that he did not have to thank me, and it was an honor. Just as I uttered those words, he vomited, and we found ourselves repeating the entire process, surely a humiliating experience for him.

After the bath, we prepared to have breakfast. He was used to us feeding him and encouraging another bite even after he said, "No more." He was never a big eater, but his appetite had decreased even more. JB began to get frustrated because he was trying to tell me something, and for once, I could not make out what it was. He kept pointing to the calendar so I would tell him what day it was. He didn't want to hear that, though. It only made him more frustrated. I tried to change the subject, but JB was not someone that you could just change the subject with. He would kindly remind you that he was not finished with the topic. Finally, he said, "Destiny." And that's my daughter, his first grand. But even then, I could not make out what she had to do with the calendar. This went on for hours. Then finally, it hit me; her graduation was coming up. I asked if he wanted to know when the graduation was. He released the biggest sigh as if he were saying, "You finally got it, you big dummy!" He would never say that to me, but that was definitely the look he gave. He was so relieved! So, I gave it to him, but he wanted more and kept pointing to the calendar. He wasn't completely satisfied until I gave him the date and explained how many more days until that date. That melted my heart. Here he was fighting for his life, but he wanted to make sure he was there at her graduation! At that point, I could imagine what those conversations with his Creator sounded like. *Precious Lord! Prepare me!*

Chapter 15

Don't Slip Away

JB made it to the graduation. He was in a wheelchair at that time and still very weak, but he made it. He was so proud of her. We all were. He was involved with whatever his kids and grandkids had going on. The family was very important to him. During that time, he was the weakest that we had seen in a long time. He could barely make his needs known, and he wasn't walking. He would still have sporadic days in which he would surprise everyone, though. He still enjoyed listening to his music in his truck on some days. Oh, I forgot to mention that he finally retired from the Cougar some years earlier. Although it was no longer operable, it was still parked in the yard. If he wasn't sitting inside his truck listening to music, he would walk around it a few times to admire it, or maybe it was to make sure we hadn't done anything to it. He built up his strength by walking around the yard with his walker until one day, he was walking like nothing happened. Now do you believe me? I kid you not; he had nine lives.

Just as soon as JB bounced back, it's like he would forget that he was ever sick. He would push it to the limits. If you didn't keep an eye on him, he would certainly drive off and woe to the person who tried to stop him. He wasn't confused, just stubborn at times. My daughter was there visiting one day, and as he sat listening to his music in his truck. My phone rang, and she on the other end panicking. She wasn't as calm as she was the night she stayed at the hospital with him. She yelled, "Ma, Dak-Dak just pulled off in the truck, and nobody else is here."

I was nearly two hours away at home, and for some reason, I couldn't seem to gather my thoughts quickly enough. I thought I was dreaming. The man was just in a wheelchair a week or so prior. All kinds of thoughts were rushing through my head. I didn't want him to hurt himself or anybody else. I m sure the music was as loud as it could go. I asked her to follow him, while I remained on the phone with her. I asked a million and one questions. I needed to know how he was driving. I was prepared to call 9-1-1 at any moment.

She answered, "He s driving better than me." Keep in mind that he had not driven a vehicle in some time. Finally, he noticed that she was following him and gave her the look of "How can I help you?" as only he could. She stated, "He sees me," as if she was a private investigator and didn't want him to notice her. He would do anything for those grandkids, so he slowly turned around and headed home. I had already alerted Earth Angel, and she was headed toward them.

I called him on the phone once he got home to tell him how much it scared us. He didn't see what the big deal was. With disgust in his voice, he agreed not to do it again. But it was clear that it was not what he wanted, and we all were making a big deal out of nothing. I can only imagine what that must have felt like for someone who escaped death's call yet still lost some form of his independence. Just to be on the safe side, the keys were put away. Earth Angel even went the extra mile to disconnect the truck's battery! He was extra hot about that. But it was for everyone s safety. He was *back!*

I could write an endless book on the memories with JB, and it would take me forty years to tell half of it. That s how long I had him with me here on earth. He made every encounter memorable. He was funny without trying to be. And he had an effortless sense of sarcasm that I inherited. By now, we had determined that no matter how bad it looked, JB would prove everybody wrong. His kidneys had begun to decline, and he was receiving dialysis at home. But his spirits remained high. If he ever complained, we all knew it was ten times worse than what he was telling us, and therefore, it was time to seek medical attention.

On Father's Day in 2019, I journeyed back to my hometown to share the day with my family. I had already picked out the perfect card to express everything that I wanted to tell JB. I had to get my acting skills together so that I could read him the card. My Earth Angel was preparing a feast and I couldn't wait to dig in. When I arrived, I realized that he was weaker than he sounded over the phone. I can't imagine what this did to his spirits because it broke a piece of our spirit every time we saw him like that. Nevertheless, I hugged him as if I hadn't seen him in years. I made sure that he could tell how excited I was to see him by the excitement in my voice. I was an actor for JB, and he supported my shenanigans. He pulled the crisp one-hundred-dollar bill out of the card and handed the card back to me. I knew what that meant! Words are important, and it was important that the card told our story. It was time for lights, cameras, and action. When I was younger, I would wonder why it took him so long to pick out birthday cards, etc. Now, as an adult, I completely understand. He and I both always made sure that it was a one-hundred-dollar bill inside the card. Five twenties would not have the same impact.

He wasn't speaking much that day, and when he tried to speak, everything came out except what he intended to say. I slowly began to read the card. I wanted to make this performance extra special by stressing each line that detailed how much he meant to me. When I finished, he smiled to let me know he was pleased. My dad had a beautiful smile.

We all headed over to the dinner table. Despite being weak, he was able to feed himself that day. Even though I hated to see his weak moments, I secretly enjoyed feeding him. That was the least I could do without compromising his dignity. Me and Earth Angel were chit-chatting over the feast when I noticed that my niece kept calling her name. Just when Earth Angel was about to correct her for interrupting, we looked up at my dad, and he was covered in his vomit. He didn't move! He didn't even blink. He didn't alarm anyone or try to remove himself from the table. In that second, my heart broke. I felt like a shell of my dad was sitting at the table. Almost like the person sitting there wasn't him at all. He was such a clean person. I knew that if he could move, he would have. If there was anything at all that he could have done, he would have. I was speechless and defeated. My heart skipped a beat, and my lungs forgot their role. If I felt that way, just imagine what was going on in his mind!

We cleaned the table as Earth Angel took him to the back to clean him up. I went outside to the rocking chair on the front porch to clear my thoughts. Now, typically, someone would join me on the porch, but this time I sat there alone, rocking and fighting back the tears. I wanted to scream! I wanted to fight! I don't know who I wanted to fight. I Just wanted to fight. I wanted to throw something! I wanted to scream choice words. I wanted to pray, but what more could I say? So many thoughts raced through my head. All I knew was that this was not fair.

Just as that thought exited my brain, my Earth Angel guided my dad outside to sit in the rocking chair next to mine. It was just like him to show up on time. She returned inside to finish cleaning. She s a busybody. Me and my dad sat there in that summer heat and rocked in silence enjoying the crisp country air. I still found myself battling tears and struggling to contain my emotions and thoughts. A sweet, still voice whispered, "He s slipping away." Even though it was a sweet voice, I just knew it had to be the devil. So I did what I had been taught to do, and I rebuked the thought! Just as I finished the rebuke, I noticed JB slowly lift his finger and point to a deer across the road eating grass. As I turned, the deer looked up at us and JB just smiled while still pointing. That gesture let me know in that second that he was still in his shell. Deer were not uncommon in our neck of the woods. Based on the way he smiled, I sometimes wonder if it was a deer that he really saw. I turned to him and said, "Do you know how much I love you?"

And just as clear as day, he replied, "DO YOU KNOW HOW MUCH I LOVE YOUUUUUU?" I put it in all caps to let you know how he stressed it. He said it as if he had been speaking all day. He said it as if he didn't have a staring contest with only God knows what just moments earlier at the table. He did not stumble with one of the words! I reassured him that I knew he loved me. So, I thought to myself for the one-hundredth time, he s back, and that alone made everything in my world tolerable!

We enjoyed the moment! The air that was initially thick when I first arrived was now thin and crisp. The heaviness had lifted. That moment was just as peaceful as the all-white attire that I chose to wear that day. That very moment was all that we were sure of. We owned it, and nothing further was promised to us. And for what it was worth, nothing else mattered. It will always be a magical memory for me! I will be thankful for it for the rest of my days. I prepared to make the journey back home.

Chapter 16

What's Left to Say... Amen?

On the Wednesday following Father s Day, I was awakened by one of my dreams. In the dream, my dad and I were in a crowded place, and he fell down onto the floor. I was rushing to get to him and yelling for everyone else to back up and give him some space. I did not help him up, but instead, I knelt beside him and began to speak in an unknown language. I jumped up out of my sleep and lay there staring at the ceiling while struggling to catch my breath for a few minutes. I thought to myself, "Wow, I have to call my dad and tell him about the dream." It was too early though, so I got dressed and headed to the gym. My plan was to call him on the way back home. It had been a busy week at work as I was prepping my team for an upcoming audit. When I returned home, I immediately logged into my computer to check in with my team and check my meetings for the day. I had every intention to do a quick login, shower, and call my dad. The phone rang and I noticed that it was my Earth Angel. I picked up the phone and said, "Please don't tell me that he fell." I was disgusted that I had forgotten to make the call during my drive home.

She replied, "No, he didn't fall, but he is not feeling well at all, and he doesn't want to go to the hospital." I asked to speak with him, and although he spoke in a whisper, which was unlike him, he wasn't confused and his voice was very clear but weak. I tried to convince him to go to the hospital and I would meet him there and stay with him. He wasn't budging. I could tell that he was over it! I thought for a split second, how the timing could not be worse because I didn't want to let my work team down. Nevertheless, I knew I had to go! My team knew I had to go and they supported me one hundred percent. Anyone who knew me knew I had to go.

I ran upstairs to grab my pre-packed overnight bag and packed all of the things that I needed for work. My youngest son was seven at the time, I quickly ensured that he had what was needed, and we hit the road. My older kids were not home , so, I called to tell them I was headed out and that I would let them know later which hospital to meet us at. It wasn't unusual for him to be transferred to a larger hospital being that he lived in a small town.

I know I must have been speeding down the highway. I didn't like the way he sounded. While driving, I called one of his sisters to let her know. She is also one of my prayer partners. I forgot that she was on vacation before calling her. After letting her know that we were headed to the hospital, something came over me. No, it wasn't like the time that I was supposed to lead the song at church. This time, I started bawling out of nowhere. I mean really bawling. My voice was trembling like I was seizing; by now, you know that this is not unusual when I cry. And I couldn't control it. There was no way that I wanted to do that to her while she was on vacation, but I couldn't stop. All I could get out was, "I m tired; I'm tired." What I was trying to say was, I m tired of seeing him like this! I m tired of him having to suffer. But none of that came out. Only "I m tired" made it past my lips.

Now my auntie is the epitome of strength! After silently listening, she asked, "What are we praying for?" meaning what are we asking God for? Her voice was beginning to tremble as well. We were always unified in what we were asking of God. The Bible says that where two or three are gathered in God's name, he is there also. We made sure that we had our two, she and I! When she said that, I sobbed harder. Of course, I wanted my dad to live forever! But if healing wasn't in the plans; it was beginning to beat us all up! We felt his pain. Watching him suffer destroyed a piece of us day by day. While still sobbing uncontrollably, I could hear them passing the phone around and everyone in the room was at a loss for words as they passed the phone to the next person.

Another aunt took the phone, as I'm sure it was her turn in the rotation, and said, "Oh, Sheila." in the most broken-hearted way possible before passing the phone yet again.

I was trying to say, "I m sorry," but nothing would come out. Finally, my male cousin took one for the team and took the phone. You know, the one that said we embarrassed the whole family at church. He calmly repeated, "It s going to be all right, Boot," until I was able to get myself together. It was like my dad himself whispered it. I apologized multiple times for crumbling on a call while they were on vacation, even though I knew it wasn't necessary as each of them stressed profusely. They all expressed how unnecessary the apology was. For the rest of the drive, I really don't remember talking to God as I had in the past. To be completely honest, I felt that I had told him everything there was to tell him. I was at a loss for words, and I was angry. My flesh whispered that my prayers were in vain anyway.

I m known to have a lot of bags with me wherever I go. Just when I think I have packed enough, I add more to it. Once we got to the hospital, I unloaded the car and headed inside. When I walked into the emergency room, I saw a shell of a person again. But this time, he was lying down. He was not responding to the nurses touching him. He didn't look up and say "Heeeeeey," with excitement as if he hadn't seen me in years. Nothing! Now I thought I had gathered myself before walking inside. But whatever had me in the car, jumped on me again as I fell into Earth Angel s arms. She s much smaller than me, but she held me as if I was a newborn baby. We stepped into the hallway, being sure not to upset him, if he could somehow hear us. The nurses strug-gled to get a blood pressure reading and start an IV. If he had been feeling like himself, he would let them have it and tell them to stop sticking him so much and just let him go home, but not this time. He didn't budge.

Once the nurses were done, I made my way to his side, leaned in, and laid my head next to his. I had to ask, "What s my name?" I had to!

And like clockwork, he whispered, "Sheila." This let me know that no matter what it looked like, he was inside of the shell. Now I don't know where the rest of the monologue came from, but I said something that I never imagined I could say. I never imagined that I would say it even if I could. I explained to him that I knew that he was tired and that I realized that he was worried about us. I explained that it was ok for him to take his rest and we would be ok. He didn't respond to that, but I knew that he heard me because he had just told me my name. He did whisper, "I love you, too," however.

There was a lot of traffic in the room with doctors, nurses, techs, etc. Although half of the family was on vacation, the ER room was still filled with friends and family. He typically had a lot of family to visit once we were in a room, but we were still in the emergency department. We all sat around chitchatting and loving on one another. The doctors were planning to transfer him to another hospital, per usual. It took them a while to com-plete the transfer paperwork. We were used to hurrying to wait, while at the hospital. I had been communicating with my older kids via phone. They were still in our hometown. They were planning to meet me at the receiving hospital which would be closer to them. But after waiting for a while, I advised them to just come on to the ER. By the time they arrived, JB was *back*. I know you are thinking, what in the world? He was greeting people by name as they entered the room and even cracked a few smiles. He lit up for those grandkids of course. They got the infamous "Heeeeeeeeeyyyyy." We were relieved.

The doctor motioned for me to come up to the nursing station. I had requested a scan due to a pocket of fluid that I had noticed on the left side of his chest. When I made it to the nursing station, he had a look on his face that I had seen so many times before. It was a look of dread. Although JB was semi-back to himself, I wasn't. I simply waved my hand as if to say, "Not today!" So, he simply pointed at the screen to show me the findings of the scan.

I was convinced by this point that his medical records must have been flagged to let them know that I was a nurse. I could tell that his left lung had collapsed and that his bodily fluids were shifting in spaces where they did not belong. It was all I could do to breathe so I couldn't engage in medical conversations at the time. I nodded at the doctor and asked, "How long before transportation arrives?" I then returned to the room to join my family. I m sure at that moment, he questioned if I was a nurse at all. Maybe he questioned if I was sane. I was neither at that time. I was simply JB s daughter. That s It!

As always, nothing about JB was textbook. His breathing wasn't labored. He didn't have any skin discolorations. I even checked his nail beds which were nice and pink. He kept his nails neatly trimmed and clean. I would catch him looking off like he was in deep thought, and I would say something really stupid to distract him; just as I did as a kid. Anything at all, like where we were going for our next trip.

Family & friends began to head out as he began to show slight progress, or should I say that he was more alert. Our immediate family stayed behind and waited for the transfer. It wasn't much longer before the ambulance arrived for it. We all hugged JB several times and assured him that we would meet him at the receiving hospital. The ambulance driver made small talk, and I asked him to take good care of my dad, and he promised us that he would. He must have seen the flag in the chart because he began to ask me about nursing. We were busy hugging on JB. We must have told him that we loved him at least ten times, and he softly whispered, "I love you too," every time, despite not being able to open his eyes hours earlier. We gathered our belongings and headed out.

My kids trailed me to the next hospital which was only about thirty minutes away. We loaded up the car with all of my bags and hit the road. As I was turning out of the hospital, I received a text from someone that I consider a sister. I saw her name come across the screen, but I decided that I would check it once I got to the hospital. Halfway to the hospital, I realized I needed to stop for snacks, anticipating the overnight night stay. Nothing had changed in this area since my youth. A girl still needed her snacks. I pulled into the convenience store. My kids followed. I m sure that they were anticipating snacks as well. We got a lot of things that we didn't need and proceeded to the checkout line.

Suddenly, my bladder felt like it was about to explode. Even though I hadn't been to the restroom since that morning when I left home, this was unusual. I have a trained bladder that is made of steel. If my aunt was there with me, she would encourage me to hold it a little while longer, while explaining how disgusting public restrooms are. But it was an emergency! Out of nowhere, it was a 9-1-1 emergency. So, I asked the clerk if there was a restroom, and she gave me a key. I thought to myself, well at least they keep it locked. My kids were looking at me, like are you sure? I had trained them what I was taught and that was to wait it out.

I honestly don't remember if the restroom was clean. I only remember trying to maintain my squat, with an urge to pray for my dad, which I did. At the time, I thought maybe it was a coping mechanism to take my mind off of the restroom, but nevertheless, I prayed. When I came out, my kids were standing in a single-file line, looking at me as if they were surprised that no one kidnapped me in the restroom. Or maybe it was a look suggesting that I had deprived them of exploring public restrooms, yet I survived. They had enough snacks in their hands to last a whole week. We paid for the groceries (because at this point, these were not snacks) and proceeded to complete the last stretch of the drive.

Once we parked at the hospital, I realized that I had not checked the text message that I received. She had sent me a Bible verse. I can't remember the verse for the life of me, but I remember it took me aback. Not in a bad way, but it made me say hmm. It s like the world paused when I read it. My kids were making small talk and gathering all my bags and the groceries of course, but it was like I was in my head with the Bible verse.

We had been to this hospital many times before, but the walk was extremely long this time. We finally reached the Intensive Care area and Earth Angel was already in the hallway waiting for us. She let us know that they were not ready yet, so we began our usual small talk. The hall seemed extremely long and empty! I had never seen this hallway empty. Earth Angel was talking but I was in my head about the Bible verse. I caught a glimpse of a doctor in a white jacket headed in our direction. He was the only person in the hallway. I never took my eyes off him, while still pondering the verse. As he was approaching us, he suddenly stopped and turned to peek at a piece of paper that he pulled from the front pocket of his lab jacket. I imagine he was verifying our family name. He immediately said, "Mrs. Bridges," and Earth Angel answered. He asked who everyone was, and she jumped into her bragging mode and introduced everyone individually. I was in one of my JB moods and had no time for chit-chat at this point, besides, I had too many bags! I wanted to say, "Come on with it Doctor," in my JB voice!

He asked if it was okay to talk to her in front of us all, and she emphasized, "Sure."

The next words I heard seemed to have taken a century to cross his lips as if our world turned into *The Matrix*. All I heard was, "I understand that Mr. Bridges *was* a DNR (Do Not Resuscitate)."

I couldn't breathe. I didn't care about what he was going to say next! I took off running in the direction that he came from with bags that seemed to be weighing me down. The hallway immediately turned into a three-mile marathon. Although it felt as if I was racing, I was moving three times slower than a turtle it seemed. It took a lifetime to reach the double doors that literally had to have only been a few feet away. I only had one ask of God at this point in my life and that was to be there when it happened. I was hoping that the doctor was wrong, and if I ran fast enough there would still be time for me to do CPR. Besides, the doctor hadn't told me anything other than his resuscitation status.

Once I reached the doors, I quickly realized that they were locked. WHY IN THE HELL WOULD THEY LOCK THE DOORS, knowing what they knew, I yelled inside my head. So, I began beating on them like a maniac. It was like an out-of-body experience. It had to have been! I knew better or did I? I wasn't raised like this, or was I? I was supposed to smile because JB thought I was too pretty to frown, and my mom taught me not to let the world see me sweat. All of that went out of the window, along with my senses. I was temporarily blinded. I couldn't smell, hear or breathe, but in some kind of way, I was running and screaming. Some guy came to the door, and I m sure he thought I was a lunatic. I thought the same thing about myself at this point.

"What's wrong?" he asked while trying to gather my things as they hit the floor. I couldn't care less about any of them at that moment.

By then, I screamed, "Where is he?"

The guy was looking at me like where is who?

I will never understand why no one prepared him before opening that door. Someone had to know that the doctor was coming to inform the family and that we needed to be let in. I decided that he didn't have the information I needed, so I kept running right past him. He could have the bags! I was screaming "Jack?" which wasn't my dad s real name, so I m sure they were wondering who Jack was. A nurse slowly approached me and wrapped her arms around my shoulders as she led me to him.

My giant lay there lifeless but still perfect. He looked so perfect in every possible way. He didn't look as if he had a single day of sickness. He didn't look deceased. His skin wasn't discolored. He was perfect. There s no other way to put it. He looked better than he did prior to leaving him with the ambulance driver.

My worst nightmare had caught up with me! I couldn't outrun it and there was no way to escape the moment. I climbed into the bed beside his lifeless body, somehow hoping that my screams would bring him back just one more time. I lifted his lifeless upper body into my arms and began to rattle out everything in my heart. For some reason, I just wanted to say "Thank you," over and over as if I had never said it before. I was stuck in a nightmare, and if only someone could just wake me up, I would call my dad and tell him all about the dream.

I needed to hear him say, "It s going to be ok, Boot." But he said nothing. He moved nothing. This time he was really just a shell. So many times, I had comforted other families through these moments, and here I was, unconsolable and unruly in a critical care unit. I wanted to scream, "What s my name, JB?" but at that moment, I wasn't even sure that *God* knew my name anymore.

We must have sat in that hospital room for at least three hours. Family and friends came from near and far to sit there with us. I don't remember much of the conversations, but we survived at that moment because of their strength. Those that were not in the room were on the phone. Different people would hold a phone to my ear to hear a message from someone on the other end, and I had no idea what they were saying. We would entertain the idea of leaving several times, yet each time, the thought of it becoming a reality would overwhelm me. So, I would settle back into my seat, resuming my gentle gestures of rubbing his hand and head, while ensuring his covers were neatly tucked. That sounds crazy, right? I didn't want to leave him alone in that hospital! He s never had to stay alone in the hospital. I was prepared to stay, that is if that guy in the hallway picked up all of the bags that I had dropped. I couldn't possibly phantom the thought of JB lying in a morgue! Not my JB! Not my giant. This time, he didn't come back! What do we say? I had nothing nice to say! Was I expected to say to Amen? I chose to say nothing.

Part II:

Life As I Have Never Known It Before

Chapter 17

Don't Let Me Die in This

We finally decided that at some point, we had to leave the hospital room, so we headed back to the family home. It was a quiet ride. I imagine no one knew what to say. What was there *to* say? I was still upset that I wasn't there the very moment he transitioned. That was all that I asked! I know with everything in me that JB was likely praying the exact opposite. He went out just as he would have wanted. He would have never wanted to die in front of us. He rarely had any private time in the hospitals, so apparently, he took advantage of the few moments he had when those that he loved the most were not around. The Holy Spirit swiftly reminded me of my time in the restroom at the store and the urgency to pray for my dad. I wholeheartedly believe that's when my JB transitioned.

Even though, at that moment, it seemed that my prayers fell on deaf ears, I began to pray for my Earth Angel. I mean, he was our dad, but she was with him from sunup until sundown. He was her husband/other half. The ride home felt as long as a trip out of state.

As we unloaded the cars and prepared to go inside, I caught a glimpse of my dad s dog. We shared an inside joke; he'd often tease me that the dog wasn't his but rather the one I left behind. He loved that dog, and that dog loved him. Mr. Black was his name. Mr. Black didn't even look up at us; he hung his head and slowly headed to the backyard. I swear it was as if he was saying, "No need to tell me. I already know." It was clear that his heart was broken as well!

When we walked inside, the air was really thick; I continuously reminded myself to breathe. I went to his favorite recliner just to double-check and make sure that he wasn't there somehow. There were still very few words exchanged. We did something that we had never done; we all gathered in the living room area, and that s where we were when the sun came up. I m sure that we all had similar thoughts, that this all had to be a dream. If we could just make it through the night, maybe, just maybe it would make more sense the next day.

Despite my heart being crushed the sun did rise as scheduled as we sat together in the living room. Our village came from near and far to show support. There was not very much time during the day that we did not have visitors. We had our moments, trust me we did, but for the most part, we were entertaining guests who showered us with love.

We kept a close eye on Earth Angel. As a matter of fact, we all kept a close eye on each other. There was very little time to get lost in our thoughts. Every night I woke up around three a.m. to make my way to the restroom. It was like clockwork. Outside of showering, this had become my fifteen minutes of grief. The restroom was probably fifteen feet from my bedroom, but it seemed that I had to walk a mile to get there. I was hoping that I would open the bedroom door and he would be kicked back on the couch, yelling at the T.V. What I would have given to hear him yell at the players. Night after night, reality would kick in after noticing that he was not there. By the time I made it to the restroom, I was as weak as water. I would get a towel to cover my face in hopes that no one could hear me falling apart. I knew that I was on borrowed time. If I took too long, I knew that Jay would be knocking on the door to see if I was ok. Yep, even at three a.m. Somehow, I needed that nightly release. It gave me just enough strength to make it until the next bathroom break. By the third night, my cover was blown.

There was so much that needed to be done and so little time to do it. Earth Angel made sure that my sister and I were involved in every detail of the funeral arrangements. She is such an amazing human being. The most difficult part for me was selecting his burial suit. He had so many of them. He took such pride in his suits, ties, and socks. It was like I could hear him saying, "No that one doesn't go with that," and we would start over from the top. It had to be perfect. As crazy as it sounds, I wanted him to be proud of the way we dressed him. His scent filled the room with each suit we pulled from the closet. It was hard for us not to put all of his favorite things in the casket with him. I've never died, so I wasn't sure what he would need. The only time he went without his baseball cap was for church service. So, we settled with ensuring that he had an eternal baseball cap placed on his head after the services! I knew that alone would make him smile. It must have taken us hours to get through that task, or at least that s how it seemed. We laughed, cried, and we laughed until we cried again! Yet, we conquered it.

The day of the funeral came way too fast. The night before, I had my usual trip to the restroom and panic began to set in. I don't think I did much sleeping at all that night. I was stuck. I honestly didn't know how I would survive the upcoming day. The thought of living the rest of my days without JB consumed me. I was emotionally paralyzed. My world was spinning out of control, and I had no way of stopping it. My worst nightmare had become an ongoing dream that I couldn't escape. I couldn't outrun the dread that was chasing me. I was in a fight with sorrow, and unfortunately, I was losing. As a matter of fact, it wasn't even a fight. I was just allowing it to slap me around, or should I say it was punching me around. It felt as if I was left with an internal bleed, and I was slowly dying on the inside. I was drowning, and there was no water around. Even if someone had thrown me a life jacket, dry land seemed too far away for me to reach it.

The next morning, I lay in bed with an emptiness that I had never experienced before. I did what JB appeared to do when he was stressed, and I turned on his favorite songs while staring at the ceiling. My phone was ringing off the hook, and texts were coming in back-to-back from my village to let me know that they would be there every step of the way. As appreciative as I was, I couldn't reply. I could only pray that my autopilot remembered to breathe. While listening to the songs, I somehow drifted back into time when I was oblivious to this type of pain. The days in which JB kept me within arm s reach in that cougar. My soul yearned for those days.

My family came in and out of the room with no words. It was almost like they took turns deciding who would come in next. I totally got it; what was there to say? Nobody had words. There was probably a slight sense of fear that I would snap or say something that I really didn't mean. Hell, I was scared that I would snap. I put the song "I've Been Loving You Too Long" by Otis Redding on repeat and ran away from it all in my thoughts. That song was one of his favorites. I knew all his favorite songs word for word. I had recited them a million times in the Cougar, but now they seemed to have a different meaning. It was like JB himself was speaking to me through his favorite songs. The words were no longer just words. They carried weight. Maybe the words carried weight for JB all along!

I guess everyone else had given up hope of getting me out of that bed; besides we were all weaker than water. Everyone except for Earth Angel, who walked in and owned the room as only she could. This was a time when I should have been dressing her. My heart desperately wanted to, but my flesh was weak. The first thing she said was, "Sheila, you gotta turn off that music." She explained how we had to get through the day.

Here was the woman I thought came to steal my daddy so many years ago; she was pouring her strength into me on the day she was to bury the main person she did life with. Her world had been turned upside down, yet she found the strength to encourage me. She held me while my emotions poured like the Nile River. I couldn't promise anyone that I would be strong—that was out of the window at this point. But I knew that I had to find the strength to show up in some kind of way. Besides, my dad taught me that I was too pretty not to smile, and my momma said that when the doors opened, I should look the part.

Your mind does weird things while you are grieving, or at least mine did. I got dressed in a black dress with huge red roses on it. I was hoping that if JB had a view from heaven, he would be able to spot me since red was his favorite color. It wasn't long before family and friends filled the house.

We loaded up the funeral cars and headed to the church. Unfortunately, I couldn't sit in the back row as we did when we were growing up. I never liked that front seat. I kept thinking, just move your feet and don't fall, Sheila. One of our past times was attending church together, sometimes on first Sundays. He was only interested in going if it was the first Sunday. I still haven t figured out the rationale for that. As we entered the doorway of the church, there was my first love lying motionless straight ahead of me. I immediately shrunk to that little girl who used to sing songs in the back row of the same church. The lyrics rang louder in my head than anything that was going on externally. It s amazing how the subconscious knows exactly what you need. As a kid, I sang just to sing along, but as it played in my head, it wasn't for show. I needed the strength of God. I needed him to hear me, and for heaven's sake, I needed him not to pass me by.

While the invisible choir in my head was having a concert and reciting everything that I needed God to know at the moment, we slowly approached the casket as a unit. We began to whisper sweet nothings while praying to God that he somehow gave JB the ability to hear our last will and testament. By now, I noticed that my body was not aligning with my thoughts. I had lost all control, and parts of my body had started to shake, with no directive from me to do so! I guess the preacher preached—I honestly couldn't tell you if he did. The undertaker went to close the casket, and simultaneously we all popped up like clockwork. The thought of that being the last time that we would lay eyes on him on earth was entirely too much to bear. We went back to square one. We lined the side of the casket once again. We ensured that his baseball cap was neatly placed on his head as he would have wanted. There would never be a good time to step away from that casket. Never! But nevertheless, we eventually forced ourselves to back away.

We loaded the cars once again to take the last ride with JB to his final resting place. I can't explain it, but just as I always did while riding with JB, I fell asleep. I will never understand how that happened. Just like in the old days! This was the last ride, and I fell asleep! Maybe this was the peace that surpasses our understanding that the Bible speaks of. We arrived at the cemetery, and I stepped out of that car as the five-year-old girl who had visited this graveyard more times than I could count. There I stood in a familiar place during unfamiliar times. This time I was a fatherless child. There was no one to dry my tears like JB could. No one there to throw me across their shoulder like a rag doll while being careful not to wake me from my sleep. JB was GONE! There was no way of denying it at this point. The thought of him meeting Jesus and gaining eternal rest consoled what was left of my heart. I also found peace in him being reunited with his mom whom he had missed for as far back as I could remember. I stood there as the remains of my first love were prepared to be lowered into the ground next to his first love—his mother. When I had the mind of a child, my prayer was to die with him. In a sense, a part of me did.

Chapter 18

Grief Is too Heavy— the Aftermath

The crowd thinned out over the next week or so. I stayed behind for a few weeks with Earth Angel. As much as I wanted to be there for her, home was also my safe place. Every single detail of that place reminded me of JB, and yet it was still my soft landing. The longer I stayed, the longer I wanted to stay. I honestly think that I was afraid to go home and face reality. The last time that I was home in Atlanta, my dad was alive.

Jay stressed, "You have to come home at some point."

Every day, my response remained consistent: "I'll be there tomorrow." When tomorrow arrived, my answer was tomorrow. I was safe under Earth Angel's wing. Immediately after the funeral, I was expecting my dad to come to me in a dream to let me know that he was okay. I am not comparing my dad to Jesus, but in my mind; if it took Jesus three days to transition, then JB should have been able to send me a sign after three days. I confided in you earlier, admitting that grief had me entertaining some irrational thoughts. This one was no different.

I finally decided that it was time for me to stop riding Earth Angel s coat tail, put on my big girl panties, and go home. Everything from that point forward was a first. To include the first time that I crossed the threshold of my home, the first shower, the first time I sat in my kitchen, etc. EVERYTHING was a first as a fatherless child.

I found myself struggling to navigate through each passing second. It felt as though a piece of my chest was missing, prompting me to constantly rub the area to reassure myself that all of me was still intact. Although my family was hurting as well, they were very attentive and went out of their way to get a temporary smile out of me. My work family sent me the most beautiful arrangement of seasonal flowers to planta memorial garden. Earth Angel came up to assist us in planting them. It was the most beautiful flower bed ever!

Everyone in the house had returned to work and/or school. The first time I found myself alone, I was at a loss as to what to do with myself. I felt that the world was moving, and no one noticed that I wasn't. It felt as though someone had pressed the fast-forward button on everyone except me. I sat on the couch while the rest of the world whirled by at an accelerated pace. I opened the window blinds so that I could see the flower bed, and I released. I mean, I really released! I didn't have to worry about smiling or how I looked to others. I sobbed profusely. I told JB that it was ok for him to go and there I was wishing he was still here. I realized that I had been sitting in the same spot all day once my family started returning home that evening. At that moment, I feared that I might not survive this. Was I losing my mind?

I had educated my patients and their families on the stages of grief so many times before. I knew that it would hurt like HELL when the time came, but I was determined that I would intentionally skip some of the stages, including the anger stage. Why would I be angry when death was a part of life? I didn't feel that it was appropriate in this setting. I was a broken shell, just like that glass door. With any sudden movement, I would be all over the floor in a billion pieces. Every morning I woke up furious that I had not dreamed about my dad, to the point that my dreams diminished altogether, which had never happened before. I was determined that I didn't want my irritability to spill over on my family, so I would sit on the side of the bed and give myself a pep talk before starting my day. Sometimes it worked and more times than not, it didn't. But every day, I attempted to show up. I smiled, and I dressed for the occasion.

The world continued to spin while I was at a standstill in my own little bubble. I felt invisible. My dad hated for me to wear makeup, which was weird to me because I had never seen my beautiful birth mom (his first wife) without it. You guessed it, he would say that I was too pretty for makeup. That was his answer to anything that he didn't want me to do. He thought his girls were the prettiest in the world, or at least that s how he made us feel. The makeup concept didn't make sense to me, however, because my mom is gorgeous. I started to wear makeup in hopes that it would give some color to the invisible person that I saw in the mirror. I guess I thought that the makeup would hide the sorrow that ran deep in my eyes.

I struggled to find some normalcy. I worked a very demanding full-time job, but it was nothing for me to get on the couch and get stuck after work. I knew that I had to do something different and fast. I needed to stay busy. I walked into the garage and there sat a machine that I had purchased for my kids to make T-shirts as a side hobby. I picked it up, not knowing much about it at all, and carried it into the house. Over the next few weeks, I started a full-time hobby of designing T-shirts. I m sure it came out of the blue for my family and friends. But it was a way to keep my mind occupied. People from my hometown showed tremendous support. They ordered those shirts like they were going out of style. Surely they thought that I had lost my mind, but they showed up in abundance. This kept me busy after work until it was time for bed. Each night I would pray that I would dream about my dad. I would get up the next day and do it all over again. I was definitely on autopilot.

The COVID pandemic hit about seven months after my dad died. By then I had learned to find something in all situations to be thankful for. I am so thankful that my dad was not hospitalized alone and unable to receive visitors while he was sick. They would probably have had to tackle him to keep him inside and away from his family. I was thankful that his transition was swift. The world faced the unimaginable, and I often think about how he would have responded to it all. He cussed a little, just a little! So, I can imagine them telling him that he couldn't see his family and him using some choice words in response. On the flip side of that, I can imagine that if one of us had it, he would have risked his own well-being to be by our side.

During the famine, those that I loved the most were trapped indoors with me. I seemed to be doing better with continuous company. I had to think of ways to keep the teenagers indoors, so we became creative with daily activities.

I remained busy with work and making shirts as well. As if that wasn't enough, I began to remodel our house room by room. We had the house built just four years prior. But I had to stay busy. I had the entire house repainted, garage floors done, hardwood extended throughout, barn doors installed—you name it, I was doing the most, as my kids would say. I m surprised that no one sat me down to say, "Look, ma am, chill out"! I can't say that I would have listened, but they could have at least tried. I turned our already new home into a newer home. I was just doing anything at that point.

My youngest son began asking for a four-wheeler. I think he was over being trapped inside of the house. I was always afraid of four-wheelers, so I blew him off by saying that I would buy it once we got three acres of land. Land that I had no intention of purchasing. He couldn't let it go; he would come home every day and ask if we had the land yet. He would pray for the land in his nightly prayers. He was determined to get that land by any means necessary. I hadn't spent much time with God during those days. Thankfully, I have always taught my kids the power of prayer, and therefore, my son would lead prayer nightly before bed and he didn't mind reminding God of what he thought he needed, which was those three acres of land.

I would look over at him in amazement. Here I was too wrapped up in heartache that I distanced myself from my Spiritual Father. The Bible says that God will use the rocks to cry out if we don't. My son was my rock that was standing in the gap and crying out for me! Even though he would benefit if God responded, he was my missing voice at the time. Maybe he was the vehicle to talk to God on my behalf during that season. It reminded me of my youth when I was crazy enough to trust God for anything, especially when praying for my dad, or should I say I was smart enough back then!

I was taking one day at a time and beginning to adjust to my new normal. I learned to put one foot in front of the other and breathe even if that meant staying busier than I needed to be. My family was my strength. It wasn't long after the lockdown lifted that nearly three acres of land basically fell into our laps. It was an offer that I could not resist in a school district that I desired. When I told my son, he didn't seem surprised at all; besides it was what he had asked for in prayer. He wasn't just asking; he believed that it would be so. He reminded me of the version of myself that I used to know. One who asked anything of God and waited with faith-filled expectations. As much as my son was praying for the land, he had moved on to the next best thing by then. I was equally excited that God s favor still dwelled within our home despite my being disconnected.

I planned to wait a few years before building a new home. Besides, I had just made our already new home new again. JB was always on my mind whether I was happy or sad. For instance, the day that I closed on the land was so exciting, but I went home to weep because I needed him there. I still longed to make him proud. I still needed to share things with him. I needed his opinion. I needed a lecture. I needed to feel the warmth of his smile. Grief has a way of sneaking in and stealing any glimpse of joy that you find. This day was no different as I crawled into bed to waddle in what would have been if JB had been there. Grief won, despite JB s voice in my head screaming, "You gotta keep going, Boot"

It wasn't long before the urge to build a new home consumed my thoughts. I confided in one of my aunts so she sent me a few links to explore floor plans. She explained that deciding on a plan could take some time. Once I began to explore the links, there was one house that was pulling at me. I just knew it was too expensive without even checking the price, so I added it to my favorites to research it later.

A few days later, my aunt sent me a text that read, "I can see you living in this house." Since I was in a season of diminished visions, I could definitely use someone else's. I had no idea that she was looking over plans as well, but she has always supported our visions. To my surprise, it was the exact house that I had added to my favorites. I found it to be eerie, to say the least. I thought, are we that much alike to pick out the same floor plan amongst thousands of homes? I quickly told myself that she was the rich auntie (that s what we all call her), and I couldn't afford the things that she could. But just to make sure I requested an estimate on the cost to build it via the website. The website would give a roundabout quote of how much it was to build the home in your area. Let s just say that I closed the computer after I got the esti-mate and immediately began to talk myself off what was a ledge of destruction. The quote was three times outside of my budget. I was appalled that I had added it to my favorites in the first place.

A few days later, while strolling through social media, I saw a picture of a guy building a house. *It was the exact same house.* I was losing it at this point, so I ran into the garage to get a second opinion from my daughter. I couldn't trust what I was seeing. Someone had to be pulling a cruel prank. My daughter confirmed that it was the same house from the website. I know that some-times social media does some weird stuff, but could it take a floor plan from a website and drop the picture of a builder building the house into my newsfeed? Ok maybe so. I reached out to the builder and he nor I could determine how the picture showed up in my newsfeed as he lived out of state, and we were not friends on the platform, nor was he running an ad.

At that point, I was like, okay, God, are you trying to get my attention? So, I sat down to have an overdue talk with him. I was straightforward in telling him what his people down here on earth were saying it would cost to build that house. I explained how that quote was not in my budget. But, even after praying about it, I couldn't shake the vision. This wasn't unusual for me; when I put my mind to something it consumes me.

I was reminded of Habakkuk 2:2 (NIV), which says, "Write down the revelation and make it plain on tablets so that a herald may run with it." I went the extra mile to order the floor plans. This was a stretch because floor plans were expensive, and I didn't have that kind of money to throw away. Once the floor plans arrived, I wrote out my vision which was not my vision after all. This vision found me, but the Bank didn't care much about whose vision it was! They insisted that I would have to sell my current home to build this new home. This was a huge blow. This was not the way I mapped out the vision in my head. But who am I to make out someone else's vision, knowing that God's thoughts are not my thoughts?

We were barely out of a famine by this point. A full-blown pandemic, and here I was talking about building a house that was outside of my planned budget range. My youngest son, you know the one who was standing in the gap, was still trying to help me figure it out. He suggested that we move home with G-Ma (Earth Angel) while we build the house. It was like the heavens spoke through him. Maybe just maybe, it was because he was still connected to God in prayer. In his innocence, he didn't consider it a big deal to pick up and move two hours away and intrude on someone else. Of course, Earth Angel thought it was an amazing idea, as well. She rearranged her whole life and said, "Come home!" Our newly renovated home sold before it ever hit the market. So, we packed up and did just that; we went home!

We had a plan! It was forecasted that it would take one year to build the home. So, we planned to intrude on Earth Angel s space for one year until it was completed. It was just like old times! We were back in our safe place, back home in the country.

My son was able to get his four-wheeler earlier than expected and enjoy it on her property. Everyone had their own space, and it kind of felt warm and fuzzy, like my favorite childhood sitcom which consisted of a blended family. This girl, who was once afraid of the dark, was now staying in her deceased father's bedroom. I was surrounded by his favorite things, including his recliner, that I could envision him sitting in. The closet smelled as if he was standing inside of it. Everything, and I do mean everything, that surrounded me, reminded me of him.

It was at that moment I realized that I was no longer afraid of the dark. I wondered if that part of me had died with my dad. I couldn't even remember when I mastered it. It was like I had passed through another dimension of my being without even noticing when it happened. By this point, I was emotionally drained. If there were a such thing as a boogie man, he would surely get a run for his money had he approached me! I was ready and prepared for war! I had experienced unimaginable hurt when that casket closed, and I was ready to unleash on anyone who wanted to wrestle. A war was raging on the inside of me that outweighed any external threat.

My vision was cloudy. Somehow, the vibrant colors that exist all looked dull and watered down. The things that were once bright now seemed dingy. Even while standing in the sun, it felt as if I was underneath a shade tree. Despite all of this, I was no longer afraid of the dark. Somehow something good came out of this. No matter how small it seemed. What was there to fear? Besides, my worst nightmare had already become a reality.

Chapter 19:

Let's go Boot

The holidays were quickly approaching, and there was no better place to be than home. In a world full of uncertainty, this was still my safe place. The kids and I took a trip for a few days to decompress. This was major because it was my first time traveling out of state with the kids alone. As weird as it sounds, that raging war on the inside of me was causing me to grow up. It felt as if I was standing on my own two feet for the first time, even though I was forty-plus years old. I was growing up! Fear no longer had permission to reside inside of me rent-free. My security blanket was gone. Even though I was a thriving adult, he was still my security, and I knew that I could fall back on him if needed. Or I could at least lean on him. In this season, it was fight or flight. Neither of which I had.

While on that trip, I realized that my marriage was falling apart. I had shed so many tears over the past year that I didn't even know how to process it. I was fresh out of tears and I wasn't interested in purchasing anymore. The land had not yet been cleared for our forever home, and I knew situations I thought would be forever were coming to an end.

I realized why God had led me back to my place of strength and security. There is an old saying that we sometimes can't see the forest for the trees. I was able to see things clearer while home, yet, it was another blow to the face. This wasn't supposed to be my reality, I thought to myself! I wasn't supposed to be single again at my age. Nevertheless, we decided to go our separate ways before the foundation of the home was even poured. I don't even remember processing it.

My cup was empty, but I appeared to be drowning. How was that possible if the cup was empty? I was standing, but barely. Once again, I felt like that shattered glass that was in a million pieces, yet I refused to fall. Somehow the pieces of glass relied on each other to avoid hitting the ground. I relied on the previous second of the day to somehow give me what was needed for the next second to remain standing. Before I knew it, my seconds added up to minutes which eventually made a day. I remembered to smile and dress to part when I stepped out. Because my daddy taught me to smile and my mom taught me that you shouldn't look like what you've been through. While others may not have been able to tell, I noticed every crack and crevice when I looked in the mirror.

I wasn't sure if grief played a part in my decisions or not, so we took our time to decide if this was a separation or a divorce after eleven years of marriage. I remained at Earth Angel s for the next six months. I knew that I was drawing my strength from her by riding her coat tail just as I had immediately following the funeral. She is the epitome of strength. I am always a stronger version of myself around her. I knew that she would catch me before I hit the ground if at all possible.

She somehow notices when others are leaning, and her presence forces you back into an upright position. I realized this was not her cross to carry. The thought of me potentially bleeding out on her haunted me. It almost felt like I was stealing from her portion of strength she had been awarded. And although she had what seemed to be a lot and was more than willing to share, I yearned for my own portion of strength.

It had been a long six months and yet the builders had not even completed framing the new home. Prices had skyrocketed and they were struggling to meet the contracted budget that was proposed before the unseen. I decided to move back to my previous city, despite my home being incomplete.

I was heavy. My spirit was heavy. My heart was heavy. For the second time in my life, I needed to see if I could fly or if I was surviving off of Earth Angel's strength. As amazing as Earth Angel is, this fight was internal. Me and the kids packed up a U-Haul and headed back. Life was becoming frustrating, but I was still determined that there were only parts of the grief process that I would allow to become my reality.

As soon as I moved back home, I realized why I felt the need to transition. I was held accountable back home. Earth Angel would not allow the bed to swallow me alive! She would step in just as she did on the day of the funeral to let me know that it was time to stand upright. She would pull me out of my thoughts by simply sitting on the side of my bed. Her presence would absorb whatever heaviness I was feeling.

I felt that my negativity was contagious, and I wasn't willing to transfer that negative energy. It belonged to me, and I needed to carry it. When I was younger, I was convinced that my sister and I were JB s strength, and now my kids returned the favor to me. I knew how to show up for them! And on the days that I struggled, they would climb in bed with me, and it would somehow restore my superpowers. They were my purpose. They were my sunshine even though the world appeared to be full of stormy days. I continued to put on a smile and show up in the world as if everything was peaches and cream. Every chance I got, I would resort back to my bed. The bed was my new best friend. She understood me! I also separated myself from those who could see beyond the smile. I knew if given the opportunity they would carry the weight if I would just set it down. My older sister was one of those people. She would pull it out of me, and therefore, I avoided her. It was too heavy for me, so I didn't want to drop it on anyone else. The little girl who was afraid of being alone now wanted to be alone all the time. I was surrounded by an army of support that I refused to use. Family and friends were still checking in daily and doing everything that they knew to do.

This was not the script that I wrote for myself. This was not the same girl who had shifted her prayers on the day of JB's death. This was not the same girl who whispered to him that we would be ok. Things were not ok, and I was mad as hell! I needed JB to call and say, "This is Jack," as if I didn't know who he was. I needed him to say, "It's gonna be ok, Boot!" I needed him to pull up and say, "Let's go!" I needed a lecture, and I promise you that I would have listened and taken notes. I longed to hear all of the things that he previously told me, just one more time. God had given me a vision of building and looking back, the plan was much bigger than a house. The project sat me down literally and caused me to be still. God was quiet, and I felt abandoned. Previously, anytime God was quiet, it meant one of two things for me:

1. Whose report will you believe? In other words, I have already told you what was to come.

2. I have equipped you to decide.

Neither of which applied in this scenario. I was in a fight with the devil, and he appeared to be winning. It seemed as if every devil imaginable revolted against it. Here I was in the midst of a vision that I didn't go looking for, and I felt like God himself vanished. I never doubted that the vision would come to pass. It had to, but I doubted that I could endure the process.

Everything that could go wrong went wrong! Even those things that couldn't go wrong went wrong. God handed me a vision, and initially, I was ready to fight with everything in me. But after a few punches, I was ready to throw in the towel and hand the vision back to him! This was for the birds and I wanted out. I felt like God had put me in the ring with every evil entity and walked away.

It was as if he thought that I was prepared for battle, and I felt that I had somehow missed the training sessions. Maybe he was standing outside of the boxing ring screaming, "Use what I have given you!" But If so, I couldn't hear his voice. If he had told me everything that came along with the vision, I would have never agreed to it. I was hurting at my core. I can't help but imagine that this must have been how JB felt when he found out I was pregnant because we had the same response: shut down. I decided that I wouldn't talk about my situation with God. Surely he knew what was going on.

I continued to pray for others, and I trusted him with everyone s problems except for my own. I would literally pray for people in the midst of conversing with them. But I was no longer praying for Sheila. I felt like he had to know what I was going through, and there was no need to keep reminding him. Especially since it was his idea. Despite it all, I never doubted the vision or who provided it. I understood Jonah from the Bible even more. I felt as if I had been swallowed by a whale while running in the wrong direction from the only person who could save me. Or perhaps I was like the disciples when Jesus took them out on the boat and it started storming. Jesus went to sleep in the middle of the storm, but at least they had enough sense to call on him and wake him up. I didn't!

I wondered where all of those people were who promised that grief would get better with time. What kind of time were they speaking of? I wanted to call them up to see if they could be more specific. I needed to gage when the heaviness in my chest would lift. Maybe they didn't know what to say and therefore they said the first thing that came to mind. Were we talking a month, a year, or ten years? Surely I should have figured this out by now. I thought that I would have adjusted to grief long before now. But honestly, my heart was still broken, and I couldn't see an end in sight. Where were the people that said that God would be a father to the fatherless. I never quite understood that saying anyway. As selfish as it sounds, I didn't care if he wasn't walking or talking; I needed my dad in any form that I could get. I knew that he would help me figure out this thing called life, and if not, he could at least set a few people straight on my behalf.

As much time as I spent in bed, my dreams still hadn't returned. Looking back, I feel like I delayed portions of the grief process by trying to avoid them, but in reality, there was no way to avoid them. Anger and some form of depression had caught up with me. Depression is deemed to be taboo in my neck of the woods and we call it everything but what it is. I was heartbroken. My heart was literally shattered. I beat myself up for being heartbroken. JB hated to see us sad and it would make him really upset. I felt like I was somehow letting him down by having a pity party after telling him that it was okay to go. I could hide my tears from everyone but myself.

JB had been gone for at least a year, yet it felt like he had taken his last breath moments ago. The "it gets better with time" slogan was not working in my favor. It had somehow forgotten about me. My time clock had stopped the moment that casket closed and I was stuck. I was suffocating!

The only person that I felt could save me was in the very cemetery that I feared since I was a kid. If only he could pull up and say, "Let's go, Boot" my world would be balanced.

When Memories Are All You Have Left

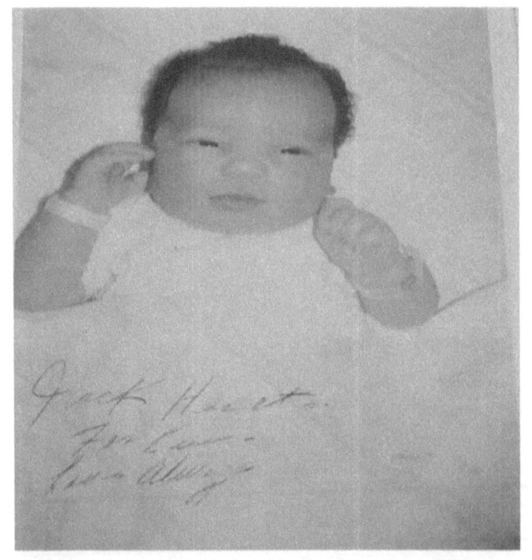

Me at birth.

The front reads:

Jack's heart forever,

Love always.

Yes, I know I was huge! I was ten lbs.

(I look five months old)

Back:

Eddie Lee Bridges

Daughter April 19th

Sheila L. Bridges

Love always, Your Father

Jack & Shirley

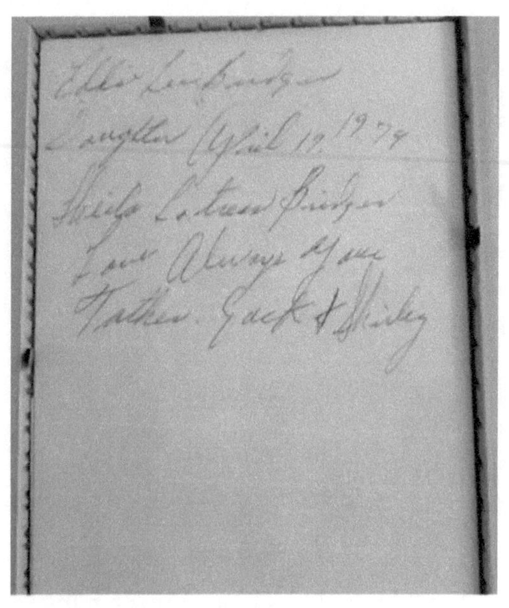

JB, my mom and their big baby!

Boot at five years old

This was the little girl who continuously called JB's office!

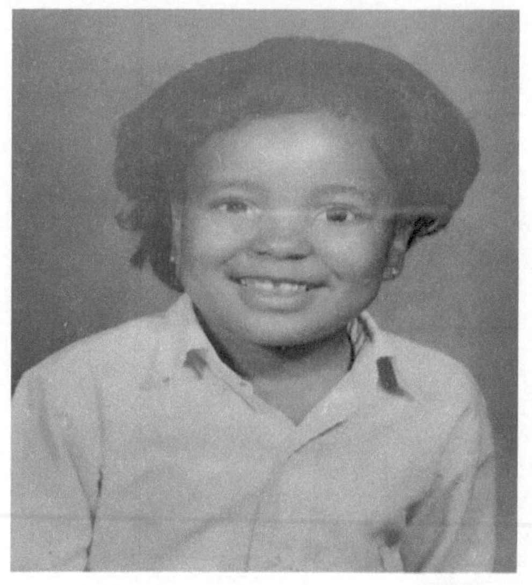

Back reads:

Jack Bridges five-year-old sweet baby.

With love always your father

Jack Bridges

(I think JB liked to write his name ☺)

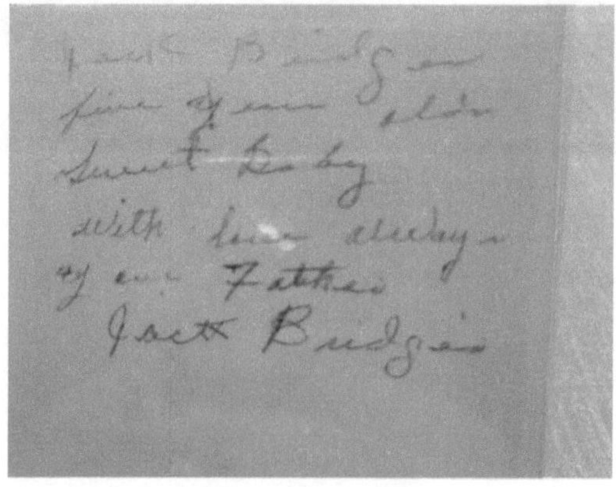

This is when the acting started. I would draw him a holiday card and after I read it to him, he would literally frame them. He never even acknowledged that I left out a *whole* word!

JB at his graduation.

World's Best
DAD

JB and Earth Angel.

JB, Earth Angel, my sister and I.

JB, Earth Angel and all of the grands.

My sister looking up at her hero.

Me headed to church only to mess up the song!
Me and my hero.

My sweet Auntie Mamie! Don't let her smile fool you; her gun was close by 😊 . My dad was her "Sam" and I was her "She-She."

The little girl that softened the giant! His first Grand, Destiny.

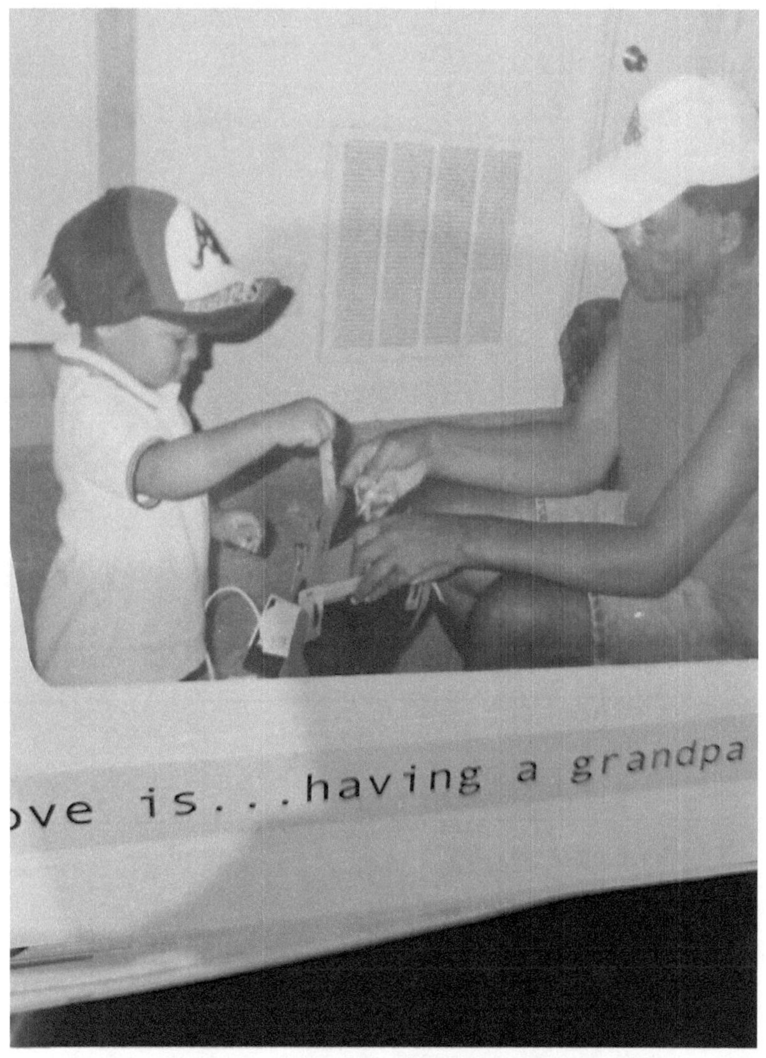

Love is ... Having a grandpa like you!

The infamous Cougar. I wonder if the Cougar made it to heaven!

Cruising—one of our favorite vacation spots.

Chapter 20

Don't Let Go

It was the summer of 2022 when things seemed to spiral. JB had been deceased for three years. You would think that I would have been well equipped by then, but I honestly think that because I kept myself busy initially, I was moving backward instead of forward. Maybe it was because life was happening, or as the kids say, "Life was Life'ing!"

Even though I had JB s lectures on repeat in my head, I needed him to hold my hand. He gave a lecture on every possible scenario that life could throw at me. Little did I know, he was downloading all the details I would need at such a time as this. I was still replaying our memories daily in my mind. I was afraid that the man that I once feared would forget me, would somehow slip away from my memory. So, to be sure that this didn't happen, I talked about him daily. I reminisced by the minute. I know those around me were sick and tired of me talking about him, but I needed to keep his memory alive. I thought I could only do this by continuously speaking his name.

I was still on strike from praying for myself! I only talked to God about other people. I rarely checked back to see if God showed up on their behalf. I would pray and leave it with God. Those were his children and I trusted him with them. My cup was officially empty, and for the first time in my life, I was comfortable letting others know it. I was respectfully releasing the title of the "strong girl." I had never asked for it, but I officially didn't want it. I was shattered but standing. Don't get me wrong, I smiled, and when I opened that door, I showed up for the world just as I had been instructed. But outside of that, I was empty.

Looking back, God had hidden me in plain sight. Or maybe I hid myself. I was surrounded in love by family and friends. I traveled a lot which gave me temporary satisfaction. Sitting beside the ocean was therapeutic for me, so I did it as often as I could. I was surrounded by people yet lonely and empty inside. It was an unimaginable and unexplainable void. It felt like I was stranded on an island surrounded by water. Or maybe, just maybe, that same fish that had swallowed Jonah had circled back for me. I was on a desolate island, yet I remained silent.

It had been 1,308 days since JB transitioned, and I finally dreamed about him. It also happened to be the day before his birthday. The timing was perfect. The dream seemed to have lasted for five years. I can remember repeating in the dream that I wasn't ready to wake up. Remember I talk to myself during my dreams.

He was sitting in the airport with his sisters when I arrived. I saw them point me out to him from afar. I ran to him at full speed as he stood there with his arms outstretched to catch me. We both fell to the floor and hugged as he wiped my tears. I told him all my worries while resting in his arms. Now my dreams are known to take weird turns. The two of us said our goodbyes to the family, and we stepped out of the airport onto an island surrounded by raging waters. In my mind this symbolized the island that I felt like I was on in real life. There was a big ship far off and JB went to get it. The huge waves were beating against him as he was trying to pull the ship to me. I could see other people on the island. I was screaming for someone to help him, but no one could hear my screams. They carried on with their business as if I didn't exist. Now, JB has always been a superhero to me, so of course he pulled the ship in. The ship was literally on his back. He fell into the sand once he reached me. I thought it killed him, but he took a deep breath just as I was waking up. I woke up weeping harder than I did at the funeral. But it wasn't a sad cry. It was a release that I had been holding in for far too long. I kept repeating "He didn't die!" I was excited that he didn't die, that meant a lot to me. Weird, right? But I woke up praising the same God that I wasn't speaking to. I was thankful to finally dream about my dad. I could write a book about what that dream meant to me alone, but I was encouraged that my ship was coming in!

It was almost a whole year later when God revealed the meaning of the dream to me. I know that I could have gotten clarity much sooner if I hadn't been stuck in my stubborn phase. My dreams slowly began to return, and for that, I was thankful.

I wish I could say that dream pulled me off that desolate island I was on, but I can't. I just knew it was the only thing I needed. For years I felt that if JB would just come to me in a dream, my world would be balanced. Don't get me wrong, it gave me a temporary gratification that I longed for, but it didn't last long enough. Despite the highs and lows, I was still determined that there was nothing left to tell God about.

As senseless as it seems, I disconnected from the source. God was a source that had been faithful to me all my life! It was the wrong timing and I've never needed to be more connected than I did in that very moment. But just like JB, I didn't want to say the wrong thing. I didn't want to come across as angry. If truth be told I *was* angry. I was confused. I was isolated and the isolation was growing by the day. It was like I was up against the giant Goliath from the Bible. At least David has a rock to fight with. I had nothing. I felt like a swing that was supposed to be connected to a tree, but unfortunately, there was a cut in the rope, and the winds were taking advantage of the disconnect. The tree never moved and was more than willing to stabilize the swing—if only it was connected.

Remember back when JB was teaching me to ride my bike, I was so afraid for him to release his hold on the bike. In my mind, I couldn't grasp why he would consider such a deadly move and release the bike. Surely, I would crash if he let go, and I knew that even as a kid. I knew how important his presence was, even if he didn't. I knew that I needed to be connected. But as an adult, here I was disconnecting from the true source. I was much smarter as a kid, apparently. My inner man was screaming, "God, please don't let go of me!" Yet the spoiled flesh was mute. Silenced!

One hot summer day, I was headed into the office just to experience some camaraderie with a few coworkers. It was one of the good days, or should I say that I was in good spirits. While working from home, I rarely got out of the house during the week, so I was excited to engage with human beings, other than my kids, of course. Don't get me wrong, I love my kids dearly. But I was overdue for interactions with other adults.

I typically use my GPS, even if I am traveling to places that I have been to a hundred times or more. With the Atlanta traffic, it s necessary, even if you are not traveling far, to avoid traffic jams. I pulled into the parking garage at work, blasting one of JB's favorite songs, such as "For the Good Times" by Al Green. I was in a zone and singing word for word. I would always lose my GPS signal once I pulled into the parking garage. This time was differ-ent. Don't get me wrong, I still lost my signal. But the GPS screamed "GPS signal lost," in a way that gripped my soul.

Now I didn't even have God on my mind during the com-mute, but it was as if the heavens opened and screamed that there was a disconnect in my prayer life! It was like someone was sitting in the car with me and shook me in an unexplainable way. When the Holy Spirit is speaking, it will use anything to grasp your attention. Now, my GPS had said this a million times before. I would usually pay it no mind because I was in the garage, and therefore, no further directives were needed. This time it gripped my spirit.

I parked the car immediately to gather my thoughts. Not only did I lose the GPS, but I also lost my satellite radio. As I sat in silence, my thoughts were all I had. The tears that I had learned to hold back flowed like the Nile River. Thank God none of my coworkers pulled up, or they would have surely thought that I had lost my mind. I didn't hear the soft still voice that I was familiar with. I heard nothing more than "GPS signal lost," honestly. However, the message was loud and clear. I took a deep breath and quickly lowered my car mirror to ensure that I put my smile back on my face, just as JB taught me. And of course, I knew how to show up for the world once that car door swung open, just as my momma demonstrated. But it was a "Wow" moment for sure and I was amazed that the heavens were still interested in little old me! Despite the number of sheep, heaven cared enough to run me down. Heaven used a simple GPS to scream "Reconnect!" as if my life depended on it. Heaven cared enough to tell me, "Don't let go! Whatever you do, don't Let Go!"

Chapter 21

Sit Down, It's Storming

My auntie Mamie attempted to teach me a valuable lesson early in life when she demanded that I be still during the storm. She would say that God was doing his work. Even as a kid, I would wonder what kind of work he was doing. What was he working on up in heaven. Was he moving furniture that caused the thunder? I didn't want to sit still long, so I was wondering if he had working hours. I wanted to know when I should expect the storm to be over. I wondered if there was a phone in heaven so that I could call and get an ETA, just as I used to do with JB's job. In this season of my life, I found myself in a storm and it wasn't even raining. This was a dry storm. And I wanted to know when I should expect it to be over. When would the brightness return to the sun? Nature had somehow lost its color and even the warmest days were cool.

Instead of being still as Auntie Mamie clearly instructed, I was busy trying to find my own way around the storm. Needless to say, I was digging a deeper hole. Not only did she tell us to be still, but she would begin to sing her hymns at that small kitchen table. Her praise would soothe my soul and before you knew it, I would fall into a deep sleep during the storm (imagine that)! Apparently, she had it all figured out. She knew to draw closer to God during the storm. Obviously, I hadn't learned anything at all from the life lessons she was teaching! Her philosophy was no different from what Psalms 46:10 explains: "Be still and know that I am God." I guess at my overgrown age, I was still somewhat of a know-it-all who really didn't know much at all. If I were wise, I would have at least cried out the words of one of those old hymns that explained everything that I needed to say.

Auntie Mamie joined the Lord about seven months before my dad. He was well enough at that time to attend the funeral. I dreamed about her while I was on this personal Island of isolation. I was running for my life in the dream. I have no idea what was chasing me. I ran into her house full speed. Of course, she was sitting at the kitchen table. I collapsed at her feet. She rose up in slow motion and pulled her pistol from the front pocket of her frock (that's what she called her house dress). She always would ensure us that she was a straight shooter and she wouldn't miss whatever it was she aimed to hit. In the dream, she only fired one shot. That was all it took. She gunned down whatever was chasing me. I was awakened by the gunshot without ever looking back.

We used to tease her about that gun. She always kept it close by. Even into my adulthood, she would reassure me that she would shoot somebody about her "She-She," as she would call me! This dream confirmed that this was spiritual warfare. The enemy knew that my grief would be an area of weakness, and he had no intentions of fighting fair. I desperately needed the whole armor of God. Whatever armor I had on at that time was simply because of grace and mercy. It certainly wasn't because of my own doing. I couldn't even call JB to tell him about the dream that I had! (Sigh). No one else would fully understand! He probably didn't understand it either, but nevertheless he listened as if he did. And he always supported the vision.

Chapter 22

Dear GOD

It wasn't long after my GPS spoke to me that I ran across a sermon, and the cliff notes were, "Sis, you need to have a one-on-one confrontation with God and tell him why you are sitting over there mad!" I thought to myself, who am I to confront the Master? I kind of dabbled in it, though. I expressed to him that I felt like he left me in the fight. A fight that I was losing. I questioned why he was quiet and reminded him of how I wanted to hold JB's hand and pray as he transitioned. It wasn't the best conversation, but it was a start. At least I was talking again. Obviously, my GPS was still disconnected because I didn't get a response. Surely, God had cut me off and wrote me out of the will, I thought.

Some of my favorite stories in the Bible were people who "questioned" God. I don't like the word confrontation per se, but take the disciples for example, when Jesus asked them to get on the boat and go to the other side of the lake. I'm sure you know the story. Remember how the storm started raging while they were out on the water? The disciples questioned Jesus. They knew where their help came from. They had witnessed numerous miracles, but they were afraid and questioned the Savior. In my mind, I can imagine them saying, "We gotta wake this man up; our lives depend on it!" Or perhaps they said, "This man is now sleeping, and we are about to die!" I'm not sure how they talked, but that's how we speak in the country.

The disciples were alarmed, and Jesus was asleep! In other words, he was quiet. I m sure they pondered before waking him, but the storm was growing stronger! Or so it seemed. I imagine Peter as the leader and going in to ask, "Jesus, do you not care if we die? We are about to drown out here, Jesus!" Instead of remaining mute, they decided to tap into the source! They knew the man who could calm the waters. I knew the man, yet here I was quietly suffering.

Another familiar challenge was when Jesus walked on water. I guess you can tell I like Peter! Peter challenged Jesus to call him out on the water. We have all heard this story a million times. But I don't recall many people focusing on the storm. The Bible said that the wind blew, and Peter lost his focus and began to sink!

The disciple who walked with Jesus lost focus because of the winds that were blowing. Despite the number of miracles he witnessed/performed, he lost focus because of a storm! However, even then, Peter was smart enough to cry out to the only hand that could save him. Yeah, I like Peter!

The last challenge I will leave you with is when Martha told Jesus that her brother would not have died had he been there. Before I found myself in a storm, I always read that verse in the most humble tone—a slight whisper, to be exact. I'm not really sure why I thought that Martha talked in a whisper. But now that my storm was raging in my head, I imagined her saying it in the same tone that I used when I reminded God that I asked to be there when JB took his last breath. I spoke out of disgust from a broken heart. Martha was disappointed and questioned the plan in a sense. I wasn't looking for similar stories to hold me up in my mess. I knew that I was wrong. But because I serve a forgiving God, he showed me that I am not the first, nor will I be the last. His grace is sufficient.

When JB wasn't speaking to me about my first pregnancy, it seemed like an eternity. It also seemed like I went an eternity without talking to God about me. As many times as God had come through for me, I can only imagine how my silence made him feel. How soon do we forget? I had disconnected from the tree of life. God favored me before I was ever born. I know this because he selected JB for me. He gave me the best person that he had in the garden to nurture and teach me. That had to be a difficult task because I am not always the easiest person to please, so I can't imagine raising me! JB made it seem easy, though. He understood me! He understood my personality. Even when he didn't quite understand me, he still showed up!

Now, remember that song we messed up in church, the one that explained that I personally needed God. You know that time when we supposedly embarrassed the whole family? I didn't understand the magnitude of that song at a young age, but I imagine that someone in the audience who was more mature than myself understood every word. I realized there comes a point when you have to step to the front of the line and say, "God, I'm praying for me this time." It had been a few weeks since I received the "GPS" revelation and the lollygag prayer I gave God to let him know how I felt. I was still heavy, very heavy!

I thought I could outsmart grief! I thought I could pick and choose what my experience would be. But now I was backed into a corner, and I was continuously regressing and revisiting stages that I once thought I had graduated from. JB was not the first person to die. As a matter of fact, he used to say, "We are all gonna have to leave here one day." in a way that only he could say it. I m sure that was something that he had to come to terms with after losing his first love, his mother. JB won t be the last person to die either, but that didn't make this burden any lighter.

I questioned everything about life after his death. I even questioned the small things, like why are we doing all of this? No matter how many things we do right, we will still die in the end. I realize that there are some things that we will never understand on this side of heaven. That s something I had to learn to accept, but first, I needed to choose survival by realizing I couldn't carry this burden alone.

I felt like Jonah in the Bible. I was somehow running in the wrong direction, and God must have created a whale to swallow me as well. Inside of the whale, I had no choice but to have a seat. Dear GOD!

Chapter 23

There Is Still So Much That Needs To Be Said

While still trapped inside the whale, I dreamed that I was pregnant. Now, that was a nightmare for me. I knew that it was something on the inside that needed to be birthed. Imagine me being too stubborn to talk to God, but he was still willing to talk to me. I was still too heavy to birth *anything*, though.

I ran across a post on social media from a friend describing a book she was reading. The book required dedicated time with

God for forty days. By now, I was desperate and I knew something had to give. I kind of viewed this as my last-ditch effort. I reached out to a friend of mine, and we committed to reading the book together. The objective of the devotion was to pray for someone else for the entire forty days. We did not know this was the objective of the book before receiving it (look at God). I had that in the bag! That was easy for me. I was already doing that. Besides, I enjoyed praying for other people, even for total strangers! Clearly, God met me where I was with this task. My friend and I exchanged our detailed prayer lists. My list was pretty generic. I was somewhat embarrassed to admit that I was still struggling with grief. I figured the rest of the world was like, "Girl, get over it" at this point.

I don't know if I took the challenge seriously because I felt that it was somewhat of a last-ditch effort for me, or if it was because I had someone else's prayers in my hands. Either way, I planned to give it all I had over the next forty days. I devoted time before daylight to meet with God while the world was yet still quiet and before I started my day. The book included daily scriptures to read as well. The goal was to give God at least forty minutes for forty days.

Initially, I thought, what in the world are we going to talk about for forty minutes? Keep in mind that I was praying for my friend, and I only knew the short prayer list she shared with me. I found myself exceeding forty minutes, not just once a day but multiple times a day. I would be out with friends and could not wait to get back home to talk to God about her prayer list. She was doing the same for me. I was eager to read my Bible to see what God wanted to say. It felt like my GPS connection had been restored. My friend was attesting to the miracles of God on her end, and it did my heart a world of good. The only concern was that God had always heard my prayers concerning others, but I wondered if I trusted him with the heavy cross I was carrying. Truth be told, his favor had always followed. Somehow, the darkness of grief had blinded me, and I could not see the forest for the trees.

God used what came naturally to get me to spend more time with him. I knew that it would take something bigger than myself, and he knew that once the commitment was made with my friend I wouldn't let her down. I was voluntarily reading my Bible more, outside of the scheduled forty minutes. The Scriptures were speaking to my every need although my friend was my focus. I started to do something that I had not previously done in my prayer life. I started to sit in silence after I finished praying. If I wanted to receive an answer, I couldn't be the one doing all the talking. I needed to hear from God. The Holy Spirit was doing just that. I was led to Scriptures and revelations like I had never experienced before. The Bible says to draw nigh unto God, and he will draw nigh unto you (James 4:8). One day, I was reading my Bible and the words, "Who touched me," literally jumped off the page at me. It was like I woke up the sleeping Giant (who was never really asleep). He had not forgotten about me despite how many other sheep he had. I, the lost sheep still mattered to him. He was patiently waiting for my return all along. I was speaking to God about my friend, and God was speaking to me about me. His revelations began to flow freely. I was ecstatic to be reconnected.

There was a song that we all sang on Auntie Mamie's porch that explained that only you and God knew about the conversations that he had with you. I sang my heart out with that song, but I must admit that it scared me as a kid. I used to think to myself, Lord, please don't crack the sky and talk to me while I'm alone. I might not be able to handle it and I might prematurely join you in heaven because of a heart attack. If he was going to talk to me, I would much rather that he did it on aunties porch so that all of us could hear it. I didn't want to be the only one. Besides I needed someone to confirm that I wasn't losing my mind if I heard from him.

I always felt safe at her house, because I knew that Auntie had that gun to protect me. My favorite cousin was always there to protect me as well. We continued to sing that song with no insight into what it actually meant. Nevertheless, we liked the sound of it. Although I was clueless as a kid, it obviously took root down on the inside of me and regurgitated itself in times such as these when the conversations with God were personal, and clearly nobody but me knew what he told me. I couldn't expect anyone else to understand the things he was revealing to me. There was so much I needed to unleash that needed to be said but that I held back on.

I began to journal and write it down. It was just like when I used to write letters to JB when I was younger. The revelations were coming back-to-back, and I learned to acknowledge the still, sweet voice of the Holy Spirit, the same voice that I rebuked on the last Father's Day that I shared with JB. I specifically recall one revelation in particular around that time. Before JB died, I loved the rain. I loved the sound of it. I loved the smell of it! I loved the sense of peace that came with it. Maybe that stemmed from Auntie Mamie demanding that we be still. After he died, rainy days were the roughest days of my life! I dreaded to see them coming. It was like all of my emotions fell from the sky during the rain. Almost as if the heavens were crying with me.

I found myself rushing in the grocery store one day. I knew that the storm was coming, and I was eager to get home beforehand. I was very impatient while in the checkout line (I got that from JB), and contemplated putting all of my items back to ensure that I made it home in time. Unfortunately, right as the cashier was trying to make small talk the bottom fell out of the sky. I was disappointed. I gathered my things to make a dash to the car. When I reached the car and unloaded my items, the Holy Spirit whispered, "You're dry." I looked and my clothes were absolutely dry. I know what you are thinking because I couldn't figure it out either. God reminded me that once I came out of this spiritual storm, I wouldn't look like what I've been though and how I am covered in his grace. I sat there in that car and enjoyed the rain on that day for the first time in years. I soaked it all in. I chose to sit still in the storm, imagine that. Auntie Mamie would be proud.

God began to use himself and JB interchangeably in my visions and dreams. I would be reminded of one of JB's lectures but God would apply it in a spiritual nature. For instance, he reminded me of how I trusted JB to hold my bike as I learned to ride. It seemed that my world was ok as long as I allowed JB to hold on to me. I felt safe in his presence. I trusted him to protect me and keep me safe, even in his weakest state. He reminded me of how I was terrified of the neighborhood dogs, but not when JB was present. I dared the dogs to chase me when JB was around. I experienced a different type of bravery just because I was next to a giant. JB would hold his arm out to motion me to stop walking and stand behind him. He would look that dog right in the eyes as if he dared him to try any funny business. It is no different when it comes to God protecting me from the enemy. But I have to trust him.

He also reminded me of the time JB expressed that he never wanted me to experience pain. God never intended for me to experience pain or death. That was not his original plan for me—for any of us! If my earthly father felt so strongly about me, imagine how God felt, the one that created both JB and I. God wanted me to trust in him wholeheartedly. There was so much that JB had to say in those repeated lectures to me. Some of them had meanings that I had yet to realize until now. There were so many ways that he expressed his unconditional love for me. I had to learn to silence my own thoughts when JB was giving instructions and recite his words that empowered me. Same with God. His directives/guidance are all in the Bible. This was his lecture to me. I just needed to silence the noise to focus on his words!

The more God revealed to me, the more I realized that there was so much that I still needed to say to God in those moments. And clearly, he was showing me that there was so much that he needed to say to me. I had longed for this type of comfort. You know, the type of comfort that gives you a peace that surpasses your understanding. I was still shattered, but I was well on my way to entertaining the idea of healing. I had reconnected with the tree of life, which in turn strengthened me daily.

The more I talked, the more God listened. The more God talked, I became eager to hear more. He dropped a bombshell on me one day during my silent moments after prayer. Remember that first dream that I had about JB? You know, the one that I waited so long to receive? It was the confirmation I longed to receive! God began to reveal the meaning of the dream almost a year later. I had not thought much about the meaning of the dream; I was just so relieved to dream about my dad.

While using the two of them interchangeably, he asked if I ever wondered why JB met me in an airport, and, of course, I didn't know. He reminded me that JB noticed me from afar in the airport and spotted his child despite the crowd and how once we reached each other, I rested in his arms for what seemed like hours. I sobbed and rested in his presence. I laid all of my worries at my daddy's feet there on the floor of the airport. God showed me that the airport represented a place to prepare for elevation. The elevation could only occur after I released and rested in my dad's (God's) arms. I was not able to move forward in the dream until I relinquished everything that I was holding inside to my father.

My daddy was willing to take that on as he whispered, "It's going to be okay, Boot." It was at that time that we got up together to leave the airport.

I reminded God that when we left the airport, we walked into a storm; as a matter of fact, we stepped out into the middle of the ocean it seemed. He reminded me that the storm did not catch him by surprise at all and that just like with Peter, he needed me to focus on him and his promises rather than the wind that was blowing and the storms.

I went on to reminisce about how in the dream, nobody could hear my desperate cries for help. He reassured me that there are times when the people around us couldn't help even if they wanted to. Elevation sometimes requires isolation. Besides, my dad never asked for help in the dream. It's up to me to believe the promise and to rely on my father. He explained that the enemy (the storm) will always show up to distract me when it's time to elevate but know that this was my daddy's (God's) battle and not mine.

JB pulled the boat onto dry land in my dream all by himself and as long as I keep my eyes on God, he will do the same. He would rescue me to dry land. I think that this was my most mind-blowing revelation to date. I know that people say not to question God, but I do, and he answers as long as I'm connected. I questioned why he held out on revealing the dream for so long, and he simply responded that I wasn't ready to receive it. My God!

Chapter 24

Don't Ever Forget Me

When JB first died, I was afraid of getting over the grief. As weird as it sounds, I wanted to feel something to ensure that I never forgot him. And if I didn't feel the pain, I felt guilty. It takes a lot of energy to love someone. What are we supposed to do with that energy once they die? I expressed that love through my love languages while he was alive, but since then, I have been left to carry it with nowhere to release it.

I thought of him constantly, reliving the memories that we once shared. I even recalled the day he died from beginning to end on a daily basis, every single second of it. I knew that people meant well by saying that it would get better with time, which it has; but I would think to myself that maybe they never lost anyone as special as JB. That was not to undermine anyone or how they felt, it's just that I felt that the pain that I felt would undoubtedly last forever! There was no way that this would ever get better. That was impossible and anyone who thought differently was foolish in my eyes. Besides, it never got better for JB when he would speak of his mom. I could still see the hurt in his eyes forty years later. At least that s what I thought. But surely it eventually became tolerable for him as well. It had to!

God has slowly begun to mend my broken heart. It still looks like a puzzle or that broken glass door, and you can clearly see where the break happened, but the gaps are not as big as they once were. Grief lies dormant for more days than before. However, there are still days that it resurfaces and the gaps in my heart are more prevalent. Psalms 34 tells me that God is close to the brokenhearted and saves those who are crushed in spirit. Maybe this is what others meant when they said God will be a father to the fatherless. I continuously remind myself of that. Maybe this is what others meant by saying that God would be a father to the fatherless. I realize that although it felt like no one in the world had felt this type of pain before, truth be told, millions experienced grief before me, and many have survived it; including JB. God loaned me someone that he treasured for forty years, and for that, I will forever be grateful. I am thankful that he knew that I would be crushed and that he promised to stay close by even though the grips of grief silenced me. Not only was he close, but he placed a hedge of protection around me.

The book of Luke in the bible reminds me that I was somewhat like the prodigal son who ran off. I had separated myself from my spiritual Father, while trying to navigate grief on my own. God and the heavens were rejoicing over my return. This particular story in the Bible tells how the father celebrated the return of his son. Even though he had a son who never left, he celebrated the return of the one that was lost. By reconnecting, I had regained access to my spiritual Father. My GPS signal was reconnected. He hears me and confirms that he hears me.

While separated the prodigal son found himself hungry and eating in places that he had no business eating. I was no different. I was hungry spiritually. There were so many advantages of the prodigal son returning home. His father's house was plentiful, and he was more than willing to feed his son's hunger with the best of his possessions. Now imagine that from a spiritual perspective. God noticed me from afar while sitting in a parking garage (JB noticed me from afar in the airport) to let me know that my inheritance was available in my Father's house, if I would just return home. It was never intended for the prodigal son to struggle and eat with pigs. And it was never intended for me to carry the burden of grief alone. Upon returning home to my Father, my low place was slowly lifting. Color was slowly returning to the things around me. The air was finally thinning out and I began to breathe without reminders.

God was JB's Father before I ever knew him, and I can only imagine how much God loved him. He had only spared his earthly life at least eighteen times. And that is double the number of lives that a cat has. I witnessed God call JB out of the grave when every doctor who touched him threw their hands in the air. I witnessed him command JB to take up his bed and walk following multiple stokes. I had witnessed him demand that his speech be returned after becoming mute. I witnessed him give him clarity during times of confusion when he couldn't even recall what year it was. I witnessed God extend his lifetime time and time again. I witnessed God give JB back to us on the day of his death, right before he was loaded into that ambulance. He ensured that all of his immediate family made it to the hospital prior to the transfer. All expressed their love. We shared a love with JB that could never die! Similar to the Bible story of Shadrach, Meshach and Abednego; God had been the fourth man in the fire for JB so many times. I witnessed miracle after miracle with my own eyes. But because of grief, I somehow neglected to remember that part.

God never promised me that JB, or anyone for that matter, would live forever on earth. But he did promise me that he would be there through it all. Psalms 147:3 tells me that he heals the broken-hearted and binds up their wounds. To date, I haven't experienced a greater pain than grief. This was a pain that only God could heal. This was a type of pain that my bones could not contain. It was deeper than the deepest parts of the sea and wider than the universe.

Despite my belief that I could skip the anger phase of grief, it didn't work. I was angry longer than I care to admit. I had to place the blame somewhere so I chose to be angry because I didn't receive confirmation that my dad was okay, but who owed me that? There I was, trying to tell God how to do his job again, but because I serve a gracious God, the Bible already told me that my dad was okay, so what difference was a dream going to make? I believed but somehow, I still needed proof via a dream. I felt that God had shown me so many things in my dreams, so why was he holding back on this one thing that I thought I desperately needed? John 11:25 tells me that those who believe in him, even though they die, they shall live. John 3:16 tells me that JB would have eternal life. I could go on and on, but you catch my drift. When we are paying attention, God is always speaking. God never promised me that JB would live forever in the flesh. But he did promise me that he would take care of him even after death. God told me what I needed in his word, the word that I chose to steer away from, but yet I wanted a sign.

God dealt with me on a personal level about how I am selective about what I trust him with. I trusted him with the issues that my family and friends endured but not my issues. I even trusted him for strangers. I trusted him time and time again to restore JB when the doctors had given up. I witnessed the miracles he performed, but now that the wind was blowing in my life, I was questioning if the miracle would happen for me, or even if those were really miracles for JB. Oh, how soon do we forget!

I was acting like the disciple Peter, after walking on water, the winds began to blow. As he lost focus, he began to sink. I also took my eyes off the source and focused on the winds that were blowing in my life. Just as God reached out his hand to save Peter, he was willing to do the same for me. I can admit, I was being a bit selective with my trust. I believed but I needed the Lord's help in my areas of unbelief (Mark 9:24). I desperately wanted to take him at all his words, for his Word shall not return to him void (Isaiah 55:11). Besides, even though I was standing, I contained a lot of broken glass within me. The were too many specs remaining within me for me to locate them all. This was impossible, but a small thing for God. JB once told me that if it was up to him, I would not know what hurt felt like. Imagine how God felt about me! He takes delight in mending my broken heart. JB kept his promise until the end that he would not forget me. I thought it was something when Earth Angel told me that I would never be too far for her to reach me, just imagine how much further my creator is willing to go. God said that he would never leave me nor forsake me, which ensures me that he will never forget me (Hebrews 13:5)! When I call, he answers!

Chapter 25:

Road to Recovery

I was having one of my "JB moments," you know, the ones in which I sit inside of my car longer than I intended to relax and gather my thoughts when the holy spirit whispered, "Write a book!"

I immediately responded, "Lord, this is Sheila." Similar to how I responded back in the day when he told me to relocate. Surely, the lines of communication had gotten crossed because I knew nothing about writing a book. There was no interest in doing one either, if I am being honest.

I thought maybe he would say, "Oh, that wasn't meant for you, Sheila." Imagine that (inserts sarcasm). But that didn't happen. When the Holy Spirit speaks to me, it's usually in very short phrases with little information at that time. The details are never given to me up front, just the end destination. Just the short and sweet, "Write a book!"

That s it? I questioned. I began to gather my things to exit the car in frustration because surely God misunderstood my prayers. Maybe he was picking up on someone else's GPS signal. While gathering my things and choosing to pretend that I didn't hear what the Holy Spirit clearly said, the title of the book dropped in my spirit instantly, *Grief Changed My DNA (Daddy's Little Girl)*. That was all I had: instructions to write a book and the title. Just those two things, and I still wasn't sold. One thing about when God speaks, he doesn't let up. The confirmations began to come back to back to remind me of my new assignment. After each confirmation (and they were coming fast), the spirit would remind me, "Write the book!"

Once I settled into the idea, or should I say the assignment, I began to question the DNA part. Initially, I got it. I knew where he was coming from or so I thought. I was a totally different person after losing JB. I had to learn myself again. My whole world was different. I was like a toddler learning to walk for the first time in a strange unfamiliar world. I was a fatherless child for the first time in my life. My outlook had changed. My thought process had changed. I still have the same bloodline, but I was definitely wired differently since he passed. But my DNA hadn't changed, not that I was aware of. Or maybe it had.

It was like I was two different people. I was the person who showed up with a smile and was well put together. On the other hand, I was a person who suffered in silence as every fiber of my being longed for my dad. Despite that, I didn't really know what God meant by DNA, but his thoughts are not my thoughts. (Isaiah 55:8-9).

It wasn't until sometime later that God dropped another bombshell. It was during prayer time that he whispered, "Daddy's not absent." I was astonished. I stood up from my chair and began to pace the room. I am not good *at all* with coming up with acronyms! I assumed that he was referring to the medical terminology DNA (deoxyribonucleic acid).

JB is not here in the natural. He has definitely gone on to be with the Lord and none of us can override that. Second Corinthians 2:8 tells me that to be absent from the body is to be present with the Lord. 1 John 4:4 lets me know that God is within me. He resides on the inside of me. He never left me! He knew what grief would look like for me. He knew that I would become angry. Nothing catches him by surprise. The Bible also tells me, "Blessed are those that mourn, for they shall be comforted" (Matthew 5:4, NIV). There was nothing that could comfort in this type of anguish but the love of God.

I am thankful that his grace and mercy covered me. Not only did he cover me and comfort me, but he also didn't let up. God has millions of sheep, yet he noticed that I was disconnected. How powerful is that? He dispatched his angels to speak to me through the GPS. THE GPS told me I needed to reconnect to the Tree of

Life to get through this. God was patiently waiting to restore my broken pieces. And trust me, there were millions of pieces. He recognizes my voice each time I call, just as JB did.

My love for JB can't compare to how much he is loved by God! That s hard for me to imagine at times. It just doesn't seem possible, but I know that it's true. JB was my earthy dad, and he was the *best* at it in my book. God is my heavenly Father. And just as God loves JB, he also loves me. JB has rescued me on countless occasions. He was a constant in all seasons of my life. On the flip side of that, God has rescued me in unimaginable ways. I m sure that I am not even aware of all the ways. The idea of him giving his only Son, so that we may have eternal life speaks to just how much he loves us. So, when God said, "Daddy's Not Absent," he wasn't only speaking of JB. He was there all along as well, even when I didn't have words for him, patiently awaiting my return! On those days I chose to shut down and climb into bed, he was right there ensuring that his grace and mercy covered me.

I can imagine him sitting on the corner of my bed on all those days when I was paralyzed by grief. I envision him reaching out his hand for me. It amazes me still how he didn't let up on me in my anguish. But I realize that would go against who he is. He promised to never leave me or forsake me. Of all his sheep that may be wandering off, he was still concerned about me.

When JB would give those lectures that I used to try to ignore, they took root inside of me, and the roots must be the size of tree trunks. Even now, no matter what I am facing, it is like the recorded version of the lecture will begin to play in my mind as if he is sitting in the room with me. It s the same with God. His Word took root in me many years ago; and no matter how far I wander off, I am reminded of his words. When I open the manual that he has provided, my strength is somehow renewed daily. When I spend quiet time with him, he speaks to my heart and comforts me!

Grief has some similarities that many of us face, for instance, the stages of grief. Those stages can look different for everyone, but one of the tricks that grief presents is the feeling that the heaviness is never ending or that you are in this alone. It s *heavy*. Very Heavy! It seems impossible. I recently visited the road that we lived on as a kid; you know, the road that my dad taught me to ride my bike on. It looked enormous, scary, and overwhelming. As a kid, I thought that it was too long/wide for me to ever make it from one end to the other. Today, it looked to be the size of a sidewalk. It literally looked like I could jump from one end of the road to the next in one jump. I wouldn't have believed you if you told me the road wasn't enormous back then.

No one can tell you what grief looks like for you. Nor can they tell you how long it will take for you to learn to navigate the waves. Just like JB was holding on to the back of my bike, God is holding on to us! He will be there even after you feel that you can balance yourself.

I have yet to determine why God asked me to write a book. I don't know if it was because he wanted me to be able to trace his tracks to show that he was there all along or if it was to help someone else understand that they are not alone in this battle against grief. Or maybe it's to show me that I need to view myself as he views me. I am yet still reminded that his thoughts are not my thoughts. I have definitely traced his steps, and therefore I have checked that box. My prayer is that it helps at least one person understand that you are not alone in the process.

Finally, I told God that I wasn't an author even after he told me to write a book. I'm learning that no matter how crazy it sounds, whatever he says is what it shall be. So if tomorrow he calls me a pilot, I suggest you hold on for the ride.

I pray that something I may have said brings an ounce of comfort to anyone who may be experiencing grief. To my sisters who may be reading this, and you have lost your earthly giant, I can relate. I can't say that I understand, but I can definitely relate. And if, by chance, this book was written to help at least one other person, I believe it to be you. We lost the one person that we needed to protect us forever, and it hurts like HELL. You may feel unprotected in a cruel, gigantic world. Greif alone feels like a never-ending burning fire! A fire that I do not suggest that you try to extinguish alone, no more than you would be expected to extinguish a burning house alone. God knew that the loss of your earthly father would leave you like shattered glass, and he is patiently waiting to put the pieces back together again.

I need you to spiritually call 9-1-1 to express the emergency that you are facing. Your earthly father poured into you tremendously, like no one else on earth could. He equipped you to keep pedaling, sis. And he left you with all the tools that he had, those that your heavenly Father equipped him with even before you were born.

That same heavenly Father has been with you all your days, and it s no different now. He knows that you are disconnected and that your heart is too heavy for you to carry. But he has sent a task force of angels to guard you and lead you back to your source of strength. Once you place your hand back in his hand, the sun will begin to shine again. You have a lot of living ahead of you! As JB would say, you must keep going. Without connecting to the Tree of Life, we simply swing in the wind, similar to the illustration on the front cover.

My prayer is that you find your spark again through Christ. Reconnect your GPS, sis! Proverbs 3:6 tells us that if we acknowledge him in all our ways, he will direct our paths. Turn by turn, he will provide directions. He is in the valley with you, waiting to lead you to the mountaintop. Starting today, I strongly urge you to spend at least five minutes with the Son and the sun. Talk to God; I promise you he talks back. You will find that you will crave more time with him after each encounter. I also want you to commit to spending time in the sun's rays. I know that it doesn't seem to shine the way it once did, but the sun's rays will gradually increase day by day! God has no respect of persons, and the same grace that was extended to me is available to you. My hope is that you look back and realize that your earthly father equipped you.

My prayer is also that you look forward with your hand in God's hand. I pray that you can hear the still voice that is speaking to you. Daddy is not absent. Your daddy is present with the Lord, who is on the inside of you. May God give you peace that surpasses your understanding. Lean onto the Tree that was created to carry your burdens for you! It's ok to put those burdens down at the base of that Tree. God is waiting to give you rest (Matthew 11:28). Chin up, sis! Know that I am rooting for you, but most importantly, know that I am praying for you!

About the Author

I'm just a daddy's girl from a small town called Milledgeville, Ga. I loved myself some JB! I experienced an unwavering type of love from my dad that shaped my entire life. He poured strength, commitment, and tenacity into me. His belief in me empowered me to achieve those things that seemed unimaginable. If I had told my dad that I wanted to fly like a bird, he would have supported it 100% because that's who he was.

I sometimes struggled seeing myself as he saw me because he saw me as unstoppable. I connected with my spiritual father at a young age by just scratching the surface. When I was a kid, we visited the local fair annually, and they gave out palm-sized bibles. As weird as it sounds that was my favorite part of the whole ordeal. I would love to sit in the corner of my room and read those words that seemed like a foreign language to me at that time, but I kept reading them anyway. I would take notes and highlight scriptures to the point that the little book was unrecognizable.

Don't get me wrong, I was no angel by far. I was a respectful spoiled brat, so don't let me reading the Bible fool you. I got away with a lot of things simply because my daddy was in the room. He didn't play about his kids. He was a gentle parent back when it was uncommon. I pushed his parenting skills to the limit. Besides receiving my annual free Bible, I enjoyed experiencing church service with my family, whether it was actual church service or the pretend services that we had on our front porch as kids. Both were equally important in my eyes. It was during those praise sessions on the front porch that I felt closer to God.

Those were the good ole days. Since then, I have experienced life lesions that were always a part of the plan, unbeknownst to me. Those experiences prepared me for days that I couldn't see coming even if I tried. Nothing could have prepared me for the death of my dad, no matter how many experiences I had beforehand. It didn't matter how many people had experienced grief before me, or how they handled it. Grief knocked me down.

I consider myself somewhat of a strong person, yet grief had me flat on my back. Had grief been willing to step into the boxing ring with me, I'm pretty sure I would have won. But unfortunately, grief doesn't fight fair, and it seems to have no sense of rules or structure. Grief sets its own set of rules, and they change without notice. Grief is a journey that many of us cannot escape. Similar to my dad, God seems to see me as unstoppable. With each passing day, I am trying to see myself as my dad once saw me. I am becoming who God reminds me that I am daily. I am learning to trust him at his word, even when I can't see the vision. This book is an example of that. Despite my own beliefs, he decided to call me an author. Watch out if he ever calls me a pilot. Thank you for exploring this journey with me.